TYPOLOGIE DES SOURCES

DU MOYEN ÂGE OCCIDENTAL

A-V.A.2*

ARS DICTAMINIS
ARS DICTANDI

UNIVERSITÉ CATHOLIQUE DE LOUVAIN

INSTITUT D'ÉTUDES MÉDIÉVALES

Collège Erasme
Place Blaise Pascal, 1
1348 LOUVAIN-LA-NEUVE (Belgique)

Conformément à la règle établie par l'Institut d'Études Médiévales, le manuscrit du présent fascicule a été soumis à un comité de lecture composé de M. J.O. Ward, Professeur à l'Université de Sydney et de MM. L. Genicot et R. Bultot, respectivement Directeur et Secrétaire de la Typologie.

TYPOLOGIE DES SOURCES
DU MOYEN ÂGE OCCIDENTAL

DIRECTEUR : L. GENICOT

Fasc. 60

A-V.A.2*

ARS DICTAMINIS
ARS DICTANDI

BY

MARTIN CAMARGO

ASSOCIATE PROFESSOR OF ENGLISH,
UNIVERSITY OF MISSOURI-COLUMBIA

BREPOLS
TURNHOUT - BELGIUM

1991

AVERTISSEMENT

Les volumes n° 58 : *Ciceronian Rhetoric in Treatise, Scholion and Commentary* de John O. WARD, n° 59 : *The Arts of Poetry and Prose* de Douglas KELLY, n° 60 : "*Ars dictaminis, Ars dictandi* " de Martin CAMARGO, ainsi que le volume à paraître ultérieurement de Marianne BRISCOE and Barbara H. JAYE : "*Artes praedicandi* " and "*Ars orandi* ", constituent un ensemble qui couvre en principe tout le champ des sources relevant de la rhétorique dans les littératures latine et vernaculaires du Moyen Age. L'équipe qui a réalisé cet ensemble a été constituée à notre demande et animée de manière exemplaire par le Professeur J.O. WARD de l'Université de Sydney. Qu'il trouve ici l'expression de notre gratitude.

Léopold GENICOT

TABLE OF CONTENTS

Bibliography 9

Chapter I : Definition of the *Ars Dictaminis* 17

Chapter II : Evolution of the Genre 29

Chapter III : Rules of Criticism 42

Chapter IV : Dissemination 47

Chapter V : Editions 51

Chapter VI : Historical Value 56

BIBLIOGRAPHY

Though a great deal of basic work remains to be done, scholarship on the *ars dictaminis* has made great strides during the last few decades. Much of this new scholarship, together with that of earlier generations, has been recorded in two bibliographical guides : James J. MURPHY, *Medieval Rhetoric : A Select Bibliography* (Toronto Medieval Bibliographies, 3), Toronto, 1971 : *The Art of Letter Writing (Ars Dictaminis)*, p. 55-70 ; 2nd ed., Toronto, 1989 : *Letter Writing : Ars dictaminis*, p. 76-103 ; and Luke REINSMA, *The Middle Ages*, in *Historical Rhetoric : An Annotated Bibliography of Selected Sources in English*, ed. Winifred Bryan HORNER, Boston, 1980, p. 43-108. Because Reinsma supplements and updates Murphy, the bibliography that follows includes only those references found neither in Murphy's nor in Reinsma's list, except for the editions of treatises on *dictamen*, which are recorded in chapter V. For a truly comprehensive guide to the scholarship, however, we must await the completion of Emil Polak's annotated bibliography of studies dealing with medieval and renaissance letter writing, comprising by Polak's current estimate over 600 entries.

The fact that the *ars dictaminis* overlaps so many other types of source material - formularies, legal tracts, *artes notariae*, grammar textbooks, etc. - poses boundary problems both in compiling a bibliography and in analyzing the genre. For example, the chapter on "Rules of Criticism" (III) below is brief because Giles Constable has already discussed the most important of those rules in his fascicle in this series dealing with yet another closely related genre, medieval letters and letter-collections. The present bibliography attempts to minimize such overlap by restricting itself to studies that deal extensively or exclusively with teachers of the *ars dictaminis*, works that call themselves *artes dictandi*, and topics, such as the *cursus*, that are inextricably associated with the *ars dictaminis*.

ALESSIO, Gian Carlo, *Brunetto Latini e Cicerone (e i Dettatori)*, in *Italia medioevale e umanistica*, 22 (1979), 123-169.

ALESSIO, Gian Carlo, *Postilla per Arsegino*, in *Storia e cultura a Padova nell'età di sant'Antonio* (Fonti e ricerche di storia ecclesiastica padovana, 16), Padua, 1985, 325-341.

AUER, Leopold, *Eine österreichische Briefsammlung aus der Zeit Friedrichs *des Streitbaren*, in *Mitteilungen des Instituts für österreichische Geschichtsforschung*, 77 (1969), 43-77.

AUER, Leopold, *Eine bisher unbekannte Handschrift des Briefstellers Bernhards von Meung*, in *Deutsches Archiv für Erforschung des Mittelalters*, 26 (1970), 230-240.

BAERWALD, Hermann, *Zur Characteristik und Kritik mittelalterlicher Formelbücher. Nach Handschriften der Wiener-Hofbibliothek*, Vienna, 1858.

BANKER, James R., *Giovanni di Bonandrea's 'Ars dictaminis' Treatise and the Doctrine of Invention in the Italian Rhetorical Tradition of the Thirteenth and Early Fourteenth Centuries*, Diss. Rochester 1972.

BENSON, Robert L., *Protohumanism and Narrative Technique in Early Thirteenth-Century Italian 'Ars Dictaminis'*, in *Boccaccio : Secoli di vita. Atti del Congresso Internazionale alla University of California-Los Angeles, 17-19 Ottobre, 1975*, a cura di Marga COTTINO-JONES e Edward F. TUTTLE (AA.VV., 4. UCLA, Center for Medieval and Renaissance Studies), Ravenna, 1979, p. 31-50.

BERTONI, Giulio, *Intorno alla vita e alle opere di Bono da Lucca*, in *Giornale storico della letteratura italiana*, 68 (1916), 161-175 ; reprinted in his *Poeti e Poesie del Medio Evo e del Rinascimento*, Modena, 1922, p. 61-81.

BEYER, Heinz-Jürgen, *Die Frühphase der 'Ars Dictandi'*, in *Studi medievali*, ser. 3, 18 (1977), 19-43.

BRESSLAU, Harry, *Handbuch der Urkundenlehre für Deutschland und Italien*, 4th ed., 2 vols, Berlin, 1968-1969.

BURDACH, Konrad, *Schlesisch-böhmische Briefmuster aus der Wende des vierzehnten Jahrhunderts*, Berlin, 1926.

CAMARGO, Martin, *Toward a Comprehensive Art of Written Discourse : Geoffrey of Vinsauf and the 'Ars dictaminis'*, in *Rhetorica*, 6 (1988), 167-194.

CAPUA, Francesco di, *Appunti sul "cursus," o ritmo prosaico, nelle opere latine di Dante Alighieri*, Castellamare, 1919 ; reprinted in his *Scritti minori*, vol. I, Rome, 1959, p. 564-585.

CAPUA, Francesco di, *Lo stile isidoriano nella retorica medievale e in Dante*, in *Studi in onore di Francesco TORRACA*, Naples, 1922, p. 233-259 ; reprinted in his *Scritti minori*, vol. II, Rome, 1959, p. 226-251.

CAPUA, Francesco di, *Il ritmo prosaico in S. Agostino*. (Estratto dalla *Miscellanea agostiniana, 2. Fuori commercio.*), Rome, 1931.

CAPUA, Francesco di, *Lo stile della Curia Romana e il 'cursus' nelle epistole di Pier della Vigna e nei documenti della cancelleria sveva*, in *Giornale Italiano di Filologia*, 2 (1944), 97-116 ; reprinted in his *Scritti minori*, vol. I, Rome, 1959, p. 500-523.

CAPUA, Francesco di, *Il "cursus" e le clausole nei prosatori latini e in Lattanzio : Corso di letteratura cristiana antica*, Bari, 1949.

CAPUA, Francesco di, *Per la storia del latino letterario medievale e del 'cursus'*, in *Giornale Italiano di Filologia*, 4 (1951), 97-113 ; reprinted in his *Scritti minori*, vol. I, Rome, 1959, p. 524-563.

CASTELLANI, Arrigo, *Le formule volgari di Guido Faba*, in *Studi di Filologia Italiana*, 13 (1955), 5-78.

DAUNOU, Pierre Claude François, *Recueil de Formules Épistolaires*, in *Histoire littéraire de la France*, vol. XIV, Paris, 1865, p. 377-381.

DAVIS, Charles T., *Brunetto Latini and Dante*, in *Studi medievali*, ser. 3, 8 (1967), 421-450.

DÜMMLER, Ernst, *Das Formelbuch des Bischofs Salemo III von Konstanz*, Leipzig, 1857.

ERDMANN, Carl, *'Leonitas'. Zur mittelalterlichen Lehre von Kursus, Rhythmus und Reim*, in *Corona quernea. Festgabe Karl STRECKER zum 80. Geburtstage dargebracht*. Schriften des Reichsinstituts für Ältere Deutsche Geschichtskunde (Monumenta Germaniae historica), 6. Leipzig, 1941 ; reprinted Stuttgart, 1952.

ERNOUT, A., *Dictāre 'Dicter', allem. Dichten*, in *Revue des Études latines*, 29e année, 1951 (Paris, 1952), 155-161.

FAULHABER, Charles B., *Retóricas clásicas y medievales en bibliotecas castellanas*, in *Ábaco*, 4 (1973), 151-300.

FAULHABER, Charles B., *Las retóricas hispanolatinas medievales siglos XII-XV*, in *Repertorio de Historia de las ciencias Eclesiásticas en España*, 7 (1979), 11-64.

FORTI, Fiorenzo, *La 'transumptio' nei dettatori bolognesi e in Dante*, in *Dante e Bologna nei tempi di Dante*, Bologna, 1967, p. 127-149.

FRATI, Carlo, *A proposito di Maestro Bene*, Rome, 1895.

FRATI, Carlo, Review of Francesco MAGGINI, *La "Rettorica" italiana di Brunetto Latini*, in *Giornale storico della letteratura italiana*, 62 (1913), 432-437.

GABRIELLI, Annibale, *Le epistole di Cola di Rienzo e l'epistolografia medievale*, in *Archivio della R. Società romana di storia patria*, 11 (1888), 381-479.

GAUDENZI, Augusto, *Lo studio di Bologna nei primi due secoli della sua esistenzia*, Bologna, 1901.

HAMPE, Karl, *Reise nach England vom Juli 1895 bis Februar 1896 : XII. Formelbücher und Briefsteller in englischen Mss*, in *Neues Archiv der Gesellschaft für ältere deutsche Geschichtskunde*, 22 (1897), 609-628.

HEATHCOTE, Sheila J., *The Letter Collections Attributed to Master Transmundus, Papal Notary and Monk of Clairvaux in the Late Twelfth Century*, in *Analecta Cisterciensia*, 21 (1965), p. 35-109, 167-238.

KALBFUSS, Hermann, *Eine Bologneser Ars dictandi des XII. Jahrhunderts*, in *Quellen und Forschungen aus italienischen Archiven und Bibliotheken*, 16, no. 2 (1914), 1-35.

KALTENBRUNNER, F., *Römische Studien III. Die Briefsammlung des Berardus de Neapoli*, in *Mitteilungen des Instituts für österreichische Geschichtsforschung*, 7 (1886), 21-118, 555-635.

KANE, Peter E., *'Dictamen' : The Medieval Rhetoric of Letter-Writing*, in *The Central States Speech Journal*, 21 (1970), 224-230.

KOLLER, Heinrich, *Zwei Pariser Briefsammlungen*, in *Mitteilungen des Instituts für österreichische Geschichtsforschung*, 59 (1951), 299-327.

KRISTELLER, Paul Oskar, *Matteo de Libri, Bolognese Notary of the Thirteenth Century and his 'Artes dictaminis'*, in *Miscellanea Giovanni GALBIATI* (Fontes Ambrosiani, 26), Milan, 1951, vol. II, p. 283-320.

LANGLOIS, Charles-Victor, *Questions d'Histoire Littéraire : Maître Bernard*, in *Bibliothèque de l'École des Chartes*, 54 (1893), 225-250.

LEGGE, M. Dominica, *William of Kingsmill – A Fifteenth-Century Teacher of French in Oxford*, in *Studies in French Language and Mediaeval Literature Presented to Professor Mildred K. POPE*, Manchester, 1939, p. 241-246.

LICITRA, Vincenzo, *Bichilino da Spello e la sua opera*, in *L'umanesimo umbro. Atti del IX Convegno di studi umbri, Gubbio 22-23 settembre 1974*, Gubbio, 1977, p. 1-21.

LICITRA, Vincenzo, *Il mito di Alberico di Montecassino iniziatore dell''Ars dictaminis'*, in *Studi medievali*, ser. 3, 18 (1977), 609-627.

LINDHOLM, Gudrun, *Studien zum mittellateinischen Prosarhythmus : Seine Entwicklung und sein Abklingen in der Briefliteratur Italiens* (Studia Latina Stockholmiensa, 10), Stockholm, 1963.

MALAGOLI, Luigi, *Forme dello stile mediolatino e forme dello stile volgare*, in *Studi Letterari. Miscellanea in onore di Emilio SANTINI*, Palermo, 1956, p. 57-86.

MARANGON, Paolo, *La 'Quadriga' e i 'Proverbi' di maestro Arsegino. Cultura e scuole a Padova prima del 1222*, in *Quaderni per la storia dell'Università di Padova*, 9-10 (1976-77), 1-44.

MARIGO, Aristide, *Il 'cursus' nella prosa latina dalle origini cristiane ai tempi di Dante*, in *Atti e Memorie della R. Accademia de Scienze, Lettere ed Arti in Padova*, n.s. 47 (1930-1931), 321-356.

MARIGO, Aristide, *Il 'cursus' nel 'De Vulgari Eloquentia' di Dante*, in *Atti e Memorie della R. Accademia de Scienze, Lettere ed Arti in Padova*, n.s. 48 (1931-1932), 85-112.

MARTI, Mario and Cesare SEGRE, *Arti del dittare, epistole e prosa d'arte*, in *La prosa del duecento* (La letteratura italiana. Storia e testi, vol. 3), Milan and Naples, 1959, p. 1-184.

MEISENZAHL, Johannes, *Die Bedeutung Bernhards von Meung für das mittelalterliche Notariats- und Schulwesen*, Diss. Würzburg, 1960.

MELLI, Elio, *I 'salut' e l'epistolografia medievale*, in *Convivium*, 30 (1962), 385-398.

MONACI, Ernesto, *Su la 'Gemma purpurea' e altri scritti volgari di Guido Faba o Fava, maestro di grammatica in Bologna nella prima metá del secolo XIII*, in *Rendiconti della Reale Accademia dei Lincei*, 4, No. 2 (1888), 299-405.

MURPHY, James Jerome, *A Fifteenth-Century Treatise on Prose Style*, in *Newberry Library Bulletin*, 6 (1966), 205-210.

OLIVAR, Marçal, *Notes entorn la influència de l''Ars dictandi' sobre la prosa catalana de cancilleria de finals del segle XIV : El Ms. Y-129-7 de la Biblioteca Colombina*, in *Estudis Universitaris Catalans*, 22 (1936), 631-653. (= *Homenatge a Antoni Rubió i Lluch. Miscellània d'estudis literaris, històrics i lingüístics*, Barcelona, 1936, vol. III, p. 631-653).

OTTO, H., *Berardus-Studien*, in *Mitteilungen des Instituts für österreichische Geschichtsforschung*, 22 (1901), 247-268.

PARODI, Ernesto Giacomo, *Intorno al testo delle epistole di Dante e al cursus*, in *Bulletino della Società Dantesca Italiana*, n.s. 19 (1912), 249-275.

PARODI, Ernesto Giacomo, *Osservazioni sul 'cursus' nelle opere latine e volgari del Boccaccio*, in *Miscellanea Storica della Valdelsa*, 21 (1913), 232-245.

PEIRONE, Luigi, *Dante, i trovatori e le 'artes dictaminis'*, in *Giornale Italiano di Filologia*, 16 (1963), 193-198.

PLEZIA, Marian, *L'origine de la théorie du 'Cursus' rhythmique au XIIe siècle*, in *Archivum Latinitatis Medii Aevi*, 39 (1974), 5-22.

QUAGLIO, Antonio Enzo, *Retorica, prosa e narrativa del Duecento* (La letteratura italiana. Storia e testi), Bari, 1970.

RICHARDSON, Henry Gerald, *An Oxford Teacher of the Fifteenth Century*, in *Bulletin of the John Rylands Library*, 23 (1939), 436-457.

RICHARDSON, Henry Gerald, *The Oxford Law School under John*, in *Law Quarterly Review*, 57 (1941), 319-338.

RICHARDSON, Henry Gerald, *Letters of the Oxford 'Dictatores'*, in *Formularies Which Bear on the History of Oxford c. 1204-1420*, eds. Herbert Edward SALTER, William Abel PANTIN, and Henry Gerald RICHARDSON, vol. II (Oxford Historical Society, n.s. 5), Oxford, 1942, p. 329-450.

ROCKINGER, Ludwig, *Ueber Formelbücher vom dreizehnten bis zum sechzehnten Jahrhundert als rechtsgeschichtliche Quellen*, Munich, 1855.

SANTI, Angelo de, *Il 'Cursus' nella storia letteraria e nella liturgia*, Rome, 1903.

SCHALK, Fritz, *Zur Entwicklung der Artes in Frankreich und Italien*, in *Artes liberales von der Antiken Bildung zur Wissenschaft des Mittelalters*, ed. Josef KOCH, Leiden, 1976, p. 137-148.

SCHALLER, Hans Martin, *Zur Entstehung der sogenannten Briefsammlung des Petrus de Vinea*, in *Deutsches Archiv*, 12 (1956), 114-159.

SCHALLER, Hans Martin, *Die Kanzlei Kaiser Friedrichs II. Ihr Personal und ihr Sprachstil. 1. Teil : Das Personal der Kanzlei*, in *Archiv für Diplomatik, Schriftgeschichte, Siegel- und Wappenkunde*, 3 (1957), 207-286.

SCHALLER, Hans Martin, *Die Kanzlei Kaiser Friedrichs II. Ihr Personal und ihr Sprachstil. 2. Teil : Der Sprachstil der Kanzlei*, in *Archiv für Diplomatik, Schriftgeschichte, Siegel- und Wappenkunde*, 4 (1958), 264-327.

SCHALLER, Hans Martin, *Studien zur Briefsammlung des Kardinals Thomas von Capua*, in *Deutsches Archiv*, 21 (1965), 371-518.

SCHALLER, Hans Martin, *Dichtungslehren und Briefsteller*, in *Die Renaissance der Wissenschaften im 12. Jahrhundert*, ed. Peter WEIMAR, Zurich, 1981, p. 249-271.

SCHIAFFINI, Alfredo, *Tradizione e poesia nella prosa d'arte italiana dalla latinità medievale al Boccaccio*, 2, Rome, 1943, 1969.

SEGRE, Cesare, *"Introduzione"* to *La prosa del duecento* (La letteratura italiana. Storia e testi, vol. 3), Milan and Naples, 1959, p. VII-XLIII ; reprinted, as *La prosa del Duecento*, in his *Lingua, stile e società. Studi sulla storia della prosa italiana*, Milan, 1963, p. 13-47.

SIMONSFELD, H., *Fragmente von Formelbüchern aus der Münchener Hof- und Staatsbibliothek*, in *Sitzungsberichte der philosophischen Classe der Akademie zu München*, Munich, 1892, p. 443-536.

SIMONSFELD, H., *Historisch-diplomatische Forschungen zur Geschichte des Mittelalters. IV. Ueber die Formelsammlung des Rudolf von Tours*, in *Sitzungsberichte der philosophisch-philologischen und der historischen Classe der königlich bayerischen Akademie der Wissenschaften zu München*, I (1898), 402-486.

SMEDICK, Lois K., *'Cursus' in Middle English : 'A Talkyng of e loue of God' Reconsidered*, in *Mediaeval Studies*, 37 (1975), 387-406.

STEHLE, Bruno, *Über ein Hildesheimer Formelbuch : Vornehmlich als Beitrag zur Geschichte des Erzbischofs Philipp I. von Köln (1167-1191)*, Sigmaringen, 1878.

TOYNBEE, Paget J. (ed., trans.), *Dantis Alagherii Epistolae*, Oxford, 1920 ; reprinted 1966. Appendix C : *Dante and the 'Cursus'*, p. 224-247.

TUNBERG, Terence O., *What Is Boncompagno's "Newest Rhetoric" ?* in *Traditio*, 42 (1986), 299-334.

UERKVITZ, Wilhelm, *Tractate zur Unterweisung in der anglonormannischen Briefschreibekunst nebst Mitteilungen aus den zugehörigen Musterbriefen*, Diss. Greifswald, 1898.

VECCHI, Giuseppe, *Giovanni del Virgilio e Dante. La polemica tra latino e volgare nella corrispondenza poetica*, in *Dante e Bologna nei tempi di Dante*, Bologna, 1967, p. 61-76.

VULLIEZ, Charles, *L'évêque au miroir de l'"ars dictaminis'. L'exemple de la 'maior compilatio' de Bernard de Meung*, in *Revue d'Histoire de l'Église de France*, 70 (1984), 277-304.

WIERUSZOWSKI, Hélène, *Beiträge zur politischen Geschichte Italiens im späteren 13. Jahrhundert (aus munizipalen 'Artes dictaminis')*, in *Quellen und Forschungen aus italienischen Archiven und Bibliotheken*, 38 (1958), 176-204 ; reprinted in her *Politics and Culture in Medieval Spain and Italy* (Storia e Letteratura, Raccolta di Studi e Testi, 121), Rome, 1971, p. 279-308.

WITT, Ronald, *Medieval 'Ars Dictaminis' and the Beginnings of Humanism : A New Construction of the Problem*, in *Renaissance Quarterly*, 35 (1982), 1-35.

WITT, Ronald, *Medieval Italian Culture and the Origins of Humanism as a Stylistic Ideal*, in *Renaissance Humanism : Foundations, Forms, and Legacy*, vol. I : *Humanism in Italy*, ed. Albert RABIL, Jr., Philadelphia, 1988, p. 29-70.

ZACCAGNINI, Guido, *Per la storia letteraria del Duecento. Notizie biografiche ed appunti dagli Archivi Bolognesi : I. Grammatici e dettatori a Bologna*, in *Il libro e la stampa*, 6 (1912), 113-160.

ZACCAGNINI, Guido, *Lettere ed orazioni di grammatici dei secc. XIII e XIV*, in *Archivum Romanicum*, 7 (1923), 517-534.

ZACCAGNINI, Guido, "*Le epistole in latino e in volgare di Pietro de' Boattieri*, in *Studi e memorie per la storia dell'Università di Bologna*, 8 (1924), 213-248.

ZACCAGNINI, Guido, *La vita dei maestri e degli scolari nello Studio di Bologna nei secoli XIII e XIV* (Biblioteca dell'*Archivum Romanicum*, ser. 1, vol. 5), Geneva, 1926.

CHAPTER I

DEFINITION OF THE *ARS DICTAMINIS*

Dictamen, from the verb *dictare* in its generalized meaning of "to compose," [1] was used during the Middle Ages to designate any type of composition. As part of the term *ars dictaminis*, however, its reference was restricted to prose composition [2]. The medieval *dictatores*, or teachers of the *ars dictaminis* frequently began their *artes dictandi*, in fact, by distinguishing among the various types of *dictamen*. They always specified at least *dictamen prosaicum* and *metricum*, more often adding *rythmicum* as a third type, and occasionally *prosimetricum* as a fourth [3]. Having excluded the other types of composition, the *dictatores* frequently went on to subdivide *dictamen prosaicum* into its various subspecies [4], from which *epistola* was then selected as the particular concern of the *ars dictaminis*. Some *dictatores* treated other types of prose composition as well [5], some even covered metrical and/or rhythmical composition together

[1] ERNOUT, *Dictāre 'Dicter,' allem. Dichten*, p. 155-161. Also see Eduard NORDEN, *Die antike Kunstprosa vom VI. Jahrhundert vor Christus bis in die Zeit der Renaissance*, 2, Leipzig, 1898, p. 953-959, and William D. PATT, *The Early 'Ars dictaminis' as Response to a Changing Society*, in *Viator*, 9 (1978), 134 n. 2 (with further references).

[2] *Dictamen* was also used as a concrete noun designating a composition that followed the rules of the *ars dictaminis*, as in Guido Faba's collection of model letters entitled *Dictamina rhetorica*. This use of the term may explain its occasional appearance in the plural in the titles of treatises that consider only one type of composition.

[3] Those who include *prosimetricum* are Hugh of Bologna, Thomas of Capua, Arsegino of Padua, Bene da Firenze, and Giovanni del Virgilio. Jacques de Dinant distinguishes seven types of *dictamen*, but in this he is unique. Emil J. POLAK, *A Textual Study of Jacques de Dinant's Summa dictaminis*, in Études de philologie et d'histoire, 28, Geneva, 1975, p. 65-66.

[4] For examples from Bernard of Bologna and Bernard de Meung, see Martin CAMARGO, *The 'Libellus de arte dictandi rhetorice' Attributed to Peter of Blois*, in *Speculum*, 59 (1984), 30. Arsegino di Padova distinguishes thirteen types (MARANGON, *Quadriga di Arsegino*, p. 40-41). Giles CONSTABLE traces the *dictatores'* practice of classifying the types of prose as far back as Sidonius' distinction between letters and history. *Letters and Letter-Collections* (Typologie des sources du moyen âge occidental, 17), Turnhout, 1976, p. 27.

[5] Bernard of Bologna is a notable example. Among his followers in the 1180s, the author of the *Libellus de arte dictandi rhetorice* retains the chapters on the other types of prose, while Bernard de Meung omits them.

with prose composition [6], but most in fact concentrated on epistolary prose.

One class of non-epistolary writings - legal documents - came to be an important part of the *ars dictaminis*, beginning with the French *dictatores* of the twelfth century. There are both theoretical and practical reasons for the inclusion of privileges, deeds, and the like in a discipline that identified its chief concern as the letter. Besides the fact that some *dictatores* might choose to view their field of expertise as prose composition in general rather than the letter in particular, the perceived gap between the legal document and the letter was not so great then as now. Medieval writers classified a much broader range of writing as epistolary than we customarily do today [7]. And even though the *dictatores* often distinguished the various types of documents from "missive" letters, even to the extent of treating them in appendices to the *ars dictandi* proper, it was clear that in form and function these public instruments were more like than unlike epistles. Most documents employed the salutation and subscription that were the least common denominator, in terms of form, of medieval letters. More important, the *dictatores* typically defined a letter as that which expresses the will of one who is not physically present and is thus unable to speak for himself. Because the bestower of a privilege or a piece of property would not be present at all times (indeed he would eventually be dead), he needed a permanent record of his intentions that could answer any challenge to the rights so bestowed. The deed "spoke for" the donor, just as a love letter spoke for the lover. Finally, the sort of people for whose training the *artes dictandi* were intended, namely, clerks and secretaries of lay and ecclesiastical chanceries, were in fact called on to produce a broad range of official documents along with what we would more strictly regard as letters. Given the quasi-public nature of all medieval letters, the distinction between personal and official correspondence, especially when produced by professional functionaries trained in the *ars dictaminis*, was in any case extremely vague [8].

[6] Most notably, John of Garland. See Traugott LAWLER, ed. and trans., *The Parisiana Poetria of John of Garland* (Yale Studies in English, 182), New Haven, 1974.

[7] *Letters and Letter-Collections*, p. 11-25.

[8] See Ronald WITT, *Boncompagno and the Defense of Rhetoric*, in *The Journal of Medieval and Renaissance Studies*, 16 (1986), p. 4: "the rules for ... official correspondence came to govern what other centuries would regard as personal letters and, consequently, with the advent of *ars dictaminis* the personal aspect of the private letter, that is, the intimate, confidential quality, the easy wandering from topic to topic, those elements which make the private letter so readable and revealing, disappeared."

The *dictatores* were not always explicit about their broader affiliations and often preferred to emphasize their autonomy [9], but when they chose to classify their field of study they consistently aligned it with rhetoric. It could be argued that the concerns of the *ars dictaminis* overlap those of the *ars grammatica* and the *ars notariae* at least as much as those of the *ars rhetorica*. Indeed, in France and England the *ars dictaminis* was generally taught by professional grammarians. The *dictatores* were justified, nonetheless, in styling themselves *rhetorici*.

The classical rhetorics, especially Cicero's *De inventione* and the pseudo-Ciceronian *Rhetorica ad Herennium*, were in fact the most important sources of dictaminal doctrine and were quoted verbatim and cited by name in many of the treatises [10]. In contrast with the medieval commentators on the Ciceronian rhetorics, the *dictatores* concerned themselves with *dispositio* and *elocutio* to the virtual exclusion of the other three parts of rhetoric [11]. That they apparently felt no incongruity in transferring precepts designed for an oral, forensic context to written texts is probably due to their perception of the letter as a species of oration [12]. Though many letters were performative or merely declarative rather than persuasive, the illusion of an oration was sustained through their standardized format, a modification of the six-part Ciceronian oration, and through the practice of reading letters aloud in public [13]. Even a work written three centuries after the first *artes dictandi* began to appear reveals a clear awareness of the oral-literate nexus at the genre's roots when it defines a letter as "not only making clear internal thoughts but also drawing the minds as much

[9] See, for example, Franz-Josef SCHMALE (ed.), Adalbertus Samaritanus, *Praecepta dictaminum*, in *MGH, Quellen zur Geistesgeschichte des Mittelalters, 3*, Weimar, 1961, p. 9-10. Boncompagno claimed, in his *Palma*, not to recall ever having "read" (i.e., lectured on) Cicero. See Carl SUTTER, *Aus Leben und Schriften des Magisters Boncompagno*, Freiburg im Breisgau, 1894, p. 105-106. In his *Rhetorica novissima*, Boncompagno asserted that the students at Bologna scorned Cicero's rhetoric: ed. Augusto GAUDENZI, in *Bibliotheca iuridica medii aevi, scripta anecdota glossatorum*, vol. 2, Bologna, 1892, p. 252b.

[10] An especially striking instance of the latter is the title of an anonymous twelfth-century treatise edited by Franz-Josef SCHMALE: *Die Precepta prosaici dictaminis secundum Tullium und die Konstanzer Briefsammlung*, Diss. Bonn, 1950.

[11] Bene da Firenze, whose *Candelabrum* treats all five parts of rhetoric, is an important exception to the rule.

[12] See especially WITT, *Medieval 'Ars Dictaminis' and the Beginnings of Humanism : A New Construction of the Problem*, p. 1-35. Witt notices a particularly strong emphasis on the controversial nature of letters among the Southern Italian *dictatores* of the thirteenth century.

[13] CONSTABLE, *Letters and Letter-Collections*, p. 13-14, 53-55, and Hans Martin SCHALLER, *Dichtungslehren und Briefsteller*, p. 256, 265.

of readers as of hearers toward the satisfying of the sender's will and pleasure" and as playing the role of a messenger ("nunciantis") "because it expresses fully the desire of the sender just as he would do were he to announce it himself or deputize someone to do so." (Thomas Merke, *Formula moderni et usitati dictaminis* (1390s), Lincoln Cathedral Library, MS 237, fols. 72r-v : "Est autem epistola nedum interiorum conceptuum explanatiua, verumeciam tam legencium quam audiencium animos ad explecionem voluntatis et beneplaciti mittentis allectiua. ... supra intencionem mittentis videtur gerere misterium nunciantis, eo quod ita plene in ea mentis explicatur effectus, sicut aliquociens faceret ipse nuncians vel delegans.")

It is probably just as significant that historically the first attempts to formulate a set of rules for the composition of letters and documents were apparently made by teachers of rhetoric. The earliest surviving remarks of the sort by a medieval writer occur in two late eleventh-century works on the traditional rhetoric of the arts curriculum by the monk Alberic of Monte Cassino. A new generation of writers, led by Adalberto Samaritano, soon stripped away much of what struck them as excess baggage to produce an art of letter writing that could stand on its own, apart from formal study of the classical *auctores*. But the *dictatores*, even when they had attained the status of a distinct faculty in thirteenth-century Bologna, recalled their rhetorical parentage long enough for the coming of humanism to invest it with new meaning [14].

The *ars dictaminis*, then, may be defined as that department of medieval rhetoric which taught the rules for composing letters and other prose documents. The vehicle for instruction in the *ars dictaminis* was the *ars* or *summa dictandi*. Although in practice the medieval authors were not so precise, a distinction will be made here between the *ars dictaminis* (discipline) and an *ars dictandi* (textbook). It will be useful to distinguish further between an *ars dictandi* and a *summa dictandi*, restricting the former to the brief, schematic tracts that summarize the theory of letter writing and illustrate it with relatively few or sometimes no complete model letters and reserving the latter for the more comprehensive works that typically begin with a theoretical *ars*, to which is appended an extensive collection of model letters and often one or more of the following as well : a rudimentary *ars notarie* or a collection of model documents,

[14] On the persistent use of classical rhetoric by even the late Italian *dictatores*, see POLAK, *Jacques de Dinant's Summa dictaminis*, p. 28-29.

a discussion of other types of prose *dictamen* besides the letter, or even an *ars rithmica*. This second distinction is more difficult to observe than the first, especially with respect to the first few works written in the genre.

From the early twelfth century through the fifteenth century, the *artes dictandi* treated much the same subjects in much the same order. Generally the treatise begins with an introduction in the form of a dedicatory epistle or a prologue, usually in prose but occasionally in verse [15]. Next, the material is divided, and important concepts, such as *dictamen*, *dictamen prosaicum*, and *epistola*, are defined. Following these preliminaries, most *artes* turn immediately to one of their two major subjects : either the rules governing prose style or, more commonly, the doctrine of letters.

Often constituting virtually the entire *ars*, the instructions on how to construct a letter are chiefly concerned with the definition, function, and arrangement of the parts of a letter. Some *dictatores* attempted to classify the various types of letters as well. None, however, discovered a systematic classification that could compel widespread acceptance, and most were content to present rules that were applicable to letters in general [16]. The *Rationes dictandi* (c. 1135) distinguished letters according to their *petitiones*, but many of its descendants revised or greatly reduced its categories [17]. One of the most practical classifications, in that it derives from the social hierarchy so crucial to the doctrine of the *salutatio*, occurs in an anonymous English treatise of the late fourteenth or early fifteenth century : "Epistolarum tres sunt species, secundum condicionem triplicem personarum. Sunt enim quedam imperatiue, quedam famuliares et quedam deprecatiue, sicut personarum quedam sunt superiores, quedam inferiores et quedam sibi inuicem equipollentes. Sunt autem epistole ad superiores personas deprecatiue, ad inferiores imperatiue, ad equipollentes famuliares." (Lincoln Cathedral Library, MS 237, fol. 64v) [18].

[15] Bernard of Bologna and Jacques de Dinant are among those who use verse prologues. Among the most important treatises, Bernard de Meung's is notable for the absence of any prologue.

[16] On the attempts at classification, see especially CONSTABLE, *Letters and Letter-Collections*, p. 21-25, and KRISTELLER, *Matteo de'Libri, Bolognese Notary of the Thirteenth Century and his 'Artes Dictaminis'*, p. 288.

[17] See CAMARGO, *'Libellus' Attributed to Peter of Blois*, p. 35, n. 65.

[18] This schema probably owes something to Hugh of Bologna's *Rationes dictandi* (ed. Ludwig ROCKINGER, *Briefsteller und Formelbücher des eilften bis vierzehnten Jahrhunderts*, Quellen und Erörterungen zur bayerischen und deutschen Geschichte, 9, no. 1 [Munich,

A consensus was more readily attained as regards the number and order of the constituent parts of a given letter. No later than 1140 the standard parts of the letter, derived from the parts of a Ciceronian oration, had become fixed at five : *salutatio*, *exordium* (also called *captatio benevolentiae* and *proverbium*), *narratio*, *petitio*, and *conclusio* [19]. Of these, the *salutatio* received the most detailed treatment, largely because of its social function. The *dictatores* emphasized the need to adapt the *salutatio* (and sometimes the rest of the letter as well) to the social status of sender and receiver. They modified the *genera dicendi* (*stilus altus*, *medius*, *humilis*) in order to devise a social hierarchy in which both secular and ecclesiastical persons were classified as *superiores/sublimi*, *pares/mediocres*, or *inferiores/infimi* [20]. The earliest *dictatores* spoke in terms of relative rather than absolute levels, [21] but very soon the social categories became fixed. Rather than formulate abstract rules to ensure that each level greeted the other decorously, most authors preferred to illustrate profusely with model salutations the full range of permutations among lay and religious senders and recipients. More than any other part of the letter, the *salutatio* thus betrays the roots of the *artes dictandi* in the formularies that had been compiled by secular and ecclesiastical secretaries since the Merovingian period [22].

The second part of a letter, as its common appellation *captatio benevolentiae* attests, served chiefly to secure the recipient's good will and thus prepare him for the message or request that followed in the *narratio*

1863 ; reprinted New York, 1961], p. 55). See also Franz QUADLBAUER, *Die antike Theorie der "genera dicendi" im lateinischen Mittelalter*, Vienna, 1962, p. 63-66.

[19] James J. MURPHY, *Rhetoric in the Middle Ages*, Berkeley, 1974, p. 224-225. The later *dictatores* were prone to increase the number of parts, usually by incorporating such physical elements of the letter as the signature and the seal. Jacques de Dinant recognizes seven parts and Thomas Sampson twelve. The opposite tendency also occurs, as in Boncompagno's attempt to reduce the number of parts to three.

[20] On these levels, see especially CONSTABLE, *The Structure of Medieval Society According to the 'Dictatores' of the Twelfth Century*, p. 253-267 ; QUADLBAUER, *"Genera dicendi" im Mittelalter*, p. 272-278 ; and Heinz-Jürgen BEYER, *Die Frühphase der 'Ars dictandi'*, p. 26-30. On the salutations in general, see the excellent study by Carol D. LANHAM, *Salutatio Formulas in Latin Letters to 1200 : Syntax, Style, and Theory* (Münchener Beiträge zur Mediävistik und Renaissance Forschung, 22), Munich, 1975.

[21] For example, Adalberto Samaritano (ed. SCHMALE, p. 33-34) and Hugh of Bologna (ed. ROCKINGER, p. 55).

[22] The formularies are covered in a separate fascicle in this series : Guido van DIEVOET, *Les Coutumiers, les Styles, les Formulaires et les "Artes notariae"* (Typologie des sources du moyen âge occidental, 48), Turnhout, 1986. Also see MURPHY, *Rhetoric in the Middle Ages*, p. 199-202.

and/or *petitio*. In discussing the means of securing good will, the *dictatores* often made superficial use of the inventional topics [23]. But as with the *salutatio*, the illustrative example is favored over the theoretical precept in most *artes*. Collections of model *exordia* and proverbs for use as *exordia* were often incorporated into the larger *summae* or copied into manuscripts along with the brief *artes* and large collections of model letters [24].

The remaining three parts generally receive far less attention than the previous two [25]. They are defined, classified, analyzed in terms of stylistic desiderata, and sometimes illustrated by an example or two. It is not unusual for the *petitio* and *conclusio* to be treated as a single part or as very closely related [26]. There is, in fact, often a final section treating the circumstances under which one or more of the standard parts may be shifted from the normal position or omitted entirely (e.g., a simple request may not require a *narratio*, while an order from a master to a servant will omit the *exordium*).

A good deal of stylistic advice is incorporated into the discussion of the various parts. The *narratio*, for example, must be *breuis*, *dilucida*, *et probabilis*, says Guido Faba and, with variations, many another [27]. In some *artes*, such brief remarks are all that is supplied by way of *elocutio* outside the models. More often, however, the subject of style is covered in some detail. Among the stylistic concerns of the *dictatores*, the rules

[23] For example, the anonymous *Rationes dictandi* (ed. ROCKINGER, *Briefsteller*, p. 18-19). Cf. Adalberto Samaritano (ed. SCHMALE, p. 57-62) and Hugh of Bologna (ed. ROCKINGER, *Briefsteller*, p. 72-81), some of whose *modi positionum* or *modi epistolarum*, respectively, resemble the *loci communes* of the classical rhetorics, but most of which seem to be stylistic devices for beginning the body of a letter. In the late twelfth and early thirteenth centuries, several *dictatores*, among them Jean de Limoges, Geoffrey of Vinsauf, and Bene da Firenze, attempted to make inventional theory a more important component of the *ars dictaminis*.

[24] KRISTELLER notes a tendency among the later dictaminal treatises to supply model *exordia* in place of full letters. "*Philosophy and Rhetoric from Antiquity to the Renaissance*," in *Renaissance Thought and Its Sources*, ed. Michael MOONEY, New York, 1979, p. 235-236. MURPHY discusses the role of proverbs in the *ars dictaminis* in *Rhetoric in the Middle Ages*, p. 233-235.

[25] As always, there are exceptions. Thomas Merke, for example, discusses the methods of abbreviating and expanding the subject matter in such great detail that the treatment of the *narratio* is the longest section of his work.

[26] As do Adalberto Samaritano, Hugh of Bologna, and the anonymous twelfth-century author of a "Flores rhetorici" in Bibliothèque Nationale, MS latin 8314, fols. 79r-83r.

[27] Augusto GAUDENZI (ed.), *Guidonis Fabe 'Summa dictaminis'*, in *Il Propugnatore*, n.s. 3, pt. 1 (1890), 332. This advice, of course, derives from the traditional Ciceronian rhetoric of the schools.

for rhythmical clause endings or *cursus* have received the most attention. Other topics that are frequently treated include the vices to be avoided and the virtues to be cultivated ; the *colores rhetorici* ; and the artful construction of clauses.

The specific *vitia* against which the prospective letter writer is warned - e.g., excessive alliteration, excessive hiatus, excessive repetition of the same word or the same ending - are chiefly taken from the *Rhetorica ad Herennium*, IV.17-18, with some additions from the grammarians. A particularly full and influential treatment of the *vitia* occurs at the beginning of Guido Faba's *Summa dictaminis* [28]. A group of more general *vitia* - *prolixitas*, *obscuritas*, *similitudo* - is often discussed as well, though usually in conjunction with the corresponding *virtutes* - *brevitas*, *claritas*, *varietas*. The ideal of *brevitas*, perhaps the most distinctive stylistic feature of the medieval *modus epistolaris*, is emphasized in virtually every extant *ars dictandi* [29]. It was considered absolutely essential in the *narratio*, but was often applied to the letter as a whole. In many of the *artes* clarity was paired with brevity, because an excess of the latter produced the vice that opposed the former [30]. The need for variety was often stated explicitly, usually supported by Cicero's dictum "similitudo mater est satietatis" (*De inventione*, I.76), but more importantly was built into the very structure of most treatises, with their collections of interchangeable model salutations, *exordia*, and the like [31]. Some *artes* conclude a discussion of the individual parts of a letter by supplying a model, each of whose parts is subsequently run through a series of variations, and most include a range of alternatives, set off by *vel*, at selected points within their model letters (especially in the *salutatio*). The principle is well illustrated in the opening of a letter adapted from Guido Faba's *dictamina*, found in Paris, Bibliothèque Nationale, MS latin 593, fol. 88r : "Mirifice bonitatis ac sapientie mulieri amice ac domine dulcissime, tali forma, sensu, et genere decorate, et oculorum suorum lumini super aurum et topazion relucenti *vel* claritate generis, forma decoris, venustate morum, et multa curialitate fulgenti *vel*

[28] *Ibid.*, p. 288-295.

[29] CONSTABLE, *Letters and Letter-Collections*, p. 19-20.

[30] For example, Alberic of Monte Cassino, *Flores rhetorici*, ed. D.M. INGUANEZ and Henry M. WILLARD (Miscellanea Cassinese, 14), Montecassino, 1938, p. 54, and Adalberto Samaritano, *Praecepta dictaminum*, ed. SCHMALE, p. 50-51.

[31] A particularly mechanical instance of this general characteristic is Lawrence of Aquilegia's *Practica sive usus dictaminis*, which converts the model letter into a series of connected slots, each to be filled from a table of options. Ed. ROCKINGER, *Briefsteller*, p. 956-966.

pre cunctis viuentibus venerande *vel* peramande, talis suus salutem et illud gaudium mentis quod voce vel actu exprimi nunquam potest *vel* tot salutes et seruicia, quot in arboribus folia, quot in celo fulgent sydera, quot in crib⟨r⟩o sunt foramina *vel* quot gutas aque continent flumina, et quot harene circa maris littora, etc. Sic me cepit vestre claritatis amor, virgo *vel* amica *vel* domina splendida, rosea et serena ...".

Although many of the *colores* are employed in the illustrative models, they are the subject of separate discussion much less frequently than the *vitia*. Several treatises, such as Bene da Firenze's, Guido Faba's, and Thomas Merke's, have extensive lists of the *colores*, complete with definitions and examples, while others treat only a few or omit them altogether. Here again the principal source is Book IV of the *Rhetorica ad Herennium*.

The doctrine of *distinctiones*, a little-studied but very important component of dictaminal style, was, like *cursus*, designed to provide a distinctive prose rhythm. Its smallest unit is the word (*dictio*), several of which form a *distinctio* or unit of thought. Several *distinctiones*, ideally three, combine to form a *clausula* or sentence. There are three varieties of *distinctio*, which are called either *distinctio suspensiva*, *distinctio constans*, and *distinctio finitiva* or, in terms borrowed from punctuation, *comma*, *colon*, and *periodus* [32]. As the first set of terms indicates, the *distinctiones* are arranged to form a pattern of tension and resolution : the first *distinctio* puts the listener in suspense and makes him wish to hear more ; the second leaves something more to be said but reveals the direction that the sentence is taking ; and the third completes the thought, leaving the listener's mind at rest. The fact that the *dictatores* generally spoke of an *auditor* rather than a *lector*, and even gave directions for pronouncing each of the three *distinctiones*, indicates that they were concerned with a rhythm both of sound and of thought [33].

Cursus, on the other hand, refers exclusively to rhythm of sound, specifically to cadences at the end (or sometimes in the middle) of *clausulae* [34]. Probably an adaptation of classical metrical clauses, which

[32] For an example of the former, see the anonymous *Rationes dictandi* (ed. ROCKINGER, *Briefsteller*, p. 25-26), for the latter, Adalberto Samaritano, *Praecepta dictaminum* (ed. SCHMALE, p. 45-46).

[33] See SCHALLER, *Dichtungslehren und Briefsteller*, p. 264-265.

[34] The *cursus* has a large bibliography. Of special value are Mathieu G. NICOLAU, *L'origine du "cursus" rythmique et les débuts de l'accent d'intensité en Latin* (Collection d'études latines, 5), Paris, 1930, and Tore JANSON, *Prose Rhythm in Medieval Latin from the Ninth to the*

were already becoming accentual in late antiquity [35], the *cursus* was not invented by the *dictatores* but was widely practiced in Europe for several centuries before formal descriptions of its rules began to appear in the French *artes dictandi* of the late twelfth century. Three types of clause ending were recommended : (1) *cursus planus*, a paroxytonic, trisyllabic word or its equivalent, preceded by a paroxytonic word (solebas ingredi) ; (2) *cursus tardus*, a proparoxytonic, tetrasyllabic word or its equivalent, preceded by a paroxytonic word (ventorum sevicia) ; and (3) *cursus velox*, a paroxytonic, tetrasyllabic word or its equivalent, preceded by a proparoxytonic word (alea constitutum). Most of the elaboration of these patterns was in spelling out the equivalents of trisyllabic and tetrasyllabic words (i.e., a monosyllable and a trisyllable count as a tetrasyllable) ; but the basic system was simple enough to be compressed into the popular mnemonic "Tris sibi similem vult, tetra sibi dissimilem vult." The French differed from the Italians in permitting some additional cadences, such as the *cursus trispondaicus* ('–/'–'–), in concerning themselves with medial as well as final cadences, and in employing the terms spondee and dactyl (to designate a paroxytone and a proparoxytone, respectively), which they borrowed from the study of metrical verse. But in most respects the rules of *cursus* were uniform throughout Europe for as long as the system was practiced and taught.

On the principle that prose should be correct as well as elegant, many *artes* also included a good deal of purely grammatical material. One type of grammatical lore that deserves special mention is called *appositio* by the early twelfth-century *Rationes dictandi* and its imitators [36]. *Appositio* is the departure from *recta constructio* or straightforward syntax, which is suitable for beginners, for the sake of more pleasing flow and sonorousness. It can also be regarded as a means of introducing variety, since many *artes* demonstrate how the same thought may be expressed elegantly in a number of different ways by changing the case of the principal noun or the form of the verb in a given *distinctio*. Thus, while there is no systematic theory of style that corresponds to the characteristic theory of structure in the *ars dictaminis* [37], there is nonetheless a considerable amount of stylistic advice in the average *ars dictandi*.

Thirteenth Century (Studia Latina Stockholmiensia, 20), Stockholm, 1975. Janson lists additional bibliography on p. 128-131.

[35] CONSTABLE, *Letters and Letter-Collections*, p. 29.

[36] Ed. ROCKINGER, *Briefsteller*, p. 26-28.

[37] MURPHY, *Rhetoric in the Middle Ages*, p. 248.

The simplest *summa dictandi* was formed by joining an *ars dictandi* of the sort just described to a collection of model letters. The need for linking precept with example, analysis of the individual elements of a letter with synthesis in the form of actual letters, was felt from the very beginning. The earliest treatises, however, tend to have fewer complete model letters than the later ones [38] and are more likely to integrate them into the body of the theoretical *ars* [39]. As time passed, the collections of model letters grew larger and more systematic and, as a result, became more sharply articulated with respect to the theoretical portion of the typical treatise. These larger collections are generally organized according to the levels of society spelled out in the chapter on the *salutatio*. Bernard de Meung's late twelfth-century collection, one of the most influential, divides several hundred letters into those sent to clergymen and those sent to laymen. Each of the two parts is further subdivided into letters sent to *superiores*, *mediocres*, and *inferiores*. As in most other collections of this sort, each letter is accompanied by its reply.

Just as *artes dictandi* continued to be produced without an accompanying letter collection throughout the history of the *ars dictaminis*, so too were there treatises on *dictamen*, such as the Roman notary Richard of Pofi's *Summa secundum stilus curie* (c. 1271), which were simply anthologies of letters classified by social levels, subject, or both [40]. Several writers achieved renown as authorities on *dictamen* because of their *epistolae*, notably Pier della Vigna and Peter of Blois. Collections of actual letters like theirs, though doubtless used for instruction in *dictamen* as similar collections were used long before the first theoretical treatises were written, should be distinguished from those collections composed by teachers of *dictamen* for the express purpose of illustrating their precepts [41]. Even when they did not form part of a *summa dictandi*, such "didactic"

[38] The *Rationes dictandi* (c. 1135) has none; its descendants the *Libellus de arte dictandi rhetorice* (1181-1185) and the "Ars dictandi aurelianensis" (1180s) each have one. I have completed an edition of the *Libellus*; for the "Ars aurelianensis," see ROCKINGER, *Briefsteller*, p. 110.

[39] For example, Adalberto Samaritano's *Praecepta dictaminum*, which concludes with ten letters but contains a number of others interspersed throughout the text. Adalberto's contemporary and rival Hugh of Bologna points the direction of the future in his *Rationes dictandi*, where all seventeen model letters are grouped at the end (ed. ROCKINGER, *Briefsteller*, p. 81-94).

[40] See Ernst BATZER, *Zur Kenntnis der Formularsammlung des Richard von Pofi* (Heidelberger Abhandlungen zur mittleren und neueren Geschichte, 28), Heidelberg, 1910.

[41] CONSTABLE, *Letters and Letter-Collections*, p. 57.

collections were almost certainly intended for use in conjunction with a theoretical text or, what amounts to the same thing, the oral lectures of a teacher.

The theoretical *ars dictandi* plus a collection of model letters formed a comprehensive manual of the *ars dictaminis*, and works of this sort are to be found from the twelfth through the fifteenth centuries. Many *dictatores* chose to expand their focus, most commonly by including a treatment of documents organized in much the same way as the *summa* just described (i.e., theoretical precepts followed by examples). Some, like Boncompagno in the thirteenth century, chose to make the various sorts of documents the subject of individual *libelli*, while others, like Bernard de Meung, incorporated such material directly into the comprehensive *summa dictandi*. Especially favored for such inclusion were privileges, though other types of documents are also considered. The treatment of documents resembles that of "missive" letters in most respects, except that considerable attention is given to the physical appearance and preparation of the documents (e.g., the type of script to be used, seals, and signatures).

With the notarial component, we exhaust those features of a *summa dictandi* that can be called typical. Since the present goal is to define the genre rather than to account for every work within it, there is no cause for listing every exception to the typical pattern. The genre was flexible enough to permit Bernard of Bologna to discuss six types of prose *dictamen* besides the letter, but only one of his many disciples chose to include that portion of Bernard's *Summa dictaminum* in his own teaching.

CHAPTER II

EVOLUTION OF THE GENRE

A systematic, comprehensive, and detailed survey of the developments that took place in the course of the *ars dictaminis*' four-hundred-year history is not yet feasible. Too many texts remain unedited, too many manuscripts imprecisely or inaccurately catalogued [42]. There have been many preliminary sketches, however, of which the fullest is the chapter on *ars dictaminis* in James J. Murphy's *Rhetoric in the Middle Ages* (p. 194-268). Murphy's survey is especially valuable for its detailed synopses of many key treatises. The briefer surveys by Hans Martin Schaller supplement Murphy's by defending a position different from his on several important issues, by filling some gaps in his coverage, and by correcting occasional errors of detail [43].

While the earliest medieval work to discuss the theory of letter writing dates from the late eleventh century, it is clear that the origins of the *ars dictaminis* lie much farther in the past. The *Ars rhetorica* (fourth century) of C. Julius Victor, which contains the earliest rhetorical treatment of letters, was apparently an anomaly. Although it anticipates such

[42] Professor Emil POLAK, Department of History, Queensborough Community College, has well under way a complete census of medieval manuscripts containing dictaminal materials. Polak has published some of his research in *Latin Epistolography of the Middle Ages and Renaissance : Manuscript Evidence in Poland*, in *Eos*, 73 (1985), 349-362. For the many editions of *artes dictandi* now in progress, see chapter V below. On the difficulty of surveying the nature and history of the *ars dictaminis*, see also David THOMSON and James J. MURPHY, *Dictamen as a Developed Genre : The Fourteenth-Century 'Brevis doctrina dictaminis' of Ventura da Bergamo*, in *Studi medievali*, ser. 3, 23 (1982), 362.

[43] SCHALLER, *Die Kanzlei Kaiser Friedrichs II. Ihr Personal und ihr Sprachstil*, pt. 2, p. 264-289, and "*Ars dictaminis, Ars dictandi*", in *Lexikon des Mittelalters*, I (1980), cols. 1034-1038. Harry BRESSLAU surveys the Italian and German materials, with emphasis on the study of documents, from the Carolingian formularies through the major *artes dictandi* to the later formularies in *Handbuch der Urkundenlehre für Deutschland und Italien*, 3d ed., Berlin, 1958, vol. 2, p. 225-281. Full of useful information, though out of date as regards their broader conclusions are Louis J. PAETOW, *The Arts Course at Medieval Universities with Special Reference to Grammar and Rhetoric*, Champaign, Ill., 1910, and Charles S. BALDWIN, *Medieval Rhetoric and Poetic (to 1400)*, New York, 1928 ; reprinted Gloucester, Mass., 1959. Max MANITIUS, *Geschichte der lateinischen Literatur des Mittelalters*, 3 vols., Munich, 1911-1931, provides concise accounts of individual authors, as do the more recent articles that Hans Martin SCHALLER has written for the *Lexikon des Mittelalters*.

dictaminal precepts as the need to be brief and to adapt the letter's tone to the social status of sender and recipient, it had little direct influence on the subsequent teaching of letter writing. During late antiquity and the early Middle Ages, one learned the art of letter writing chiefly by imitating the productions of acknowledged masters, such as Cassiodorus [44]. This sort of *imitatio* never died out completely, as the popularity of Peter of Blois' and Pier della Vigna's *epistolae* attests, and was enthusiastically revived in the humanists' cultivation of Cicero. By the Carolingian period, however, a movement toward formalization and schematization can be observed in the formularies compiled by both lay and ecclesiastical secretaries. There may also have developed by the tenth century some form of rhetoric-based instruction in letter writing, since letters clearly employing the distinctive five-part schema of the *artes dictandi* survive from that period [45]. Much has obviously been lost, and much was probably never written down ; but enough is known to demonstrate that the doctrine of the *dictatores* was observed in practice for a long time, perhaps several centuries, before it was set down in the treatises that have survived.

The debate about who was the rightful "father" of the *ars dictaminis* is therefore pointless [46]. We shall never know the extent to which the earliest surviving discussions of its rules are original or reflect an existing tradition whose records are for the most part lost. It does appear that the first medieval rhetoric treatises to give extensive coverage to the principles of letter writing, because they are not themselves comprehensive, presume on the part of their audience a prior knowledge of the subject [47]. It is equally clear that Alberic of Monte Cassino's *Breviarium de dictamine* and *Dictaminum radii* (or *Flores rhetorici*) are not *artes dictandi* of the sort defined in the previous chapter. Alberic's subject is the traditional

[44] MURPHY, *Rhetoric in the Middle Ages*, p. 195-199.

[45] KRISTELLER, *Philosophy and Rhetoric*, p. 230, 233.

[46] PATT, *The Early "Ars dictaminis" as Response to a Changing Society*, p. 133-155. CONSTABLE, *Letters and Letter-Collections*, p. 34-35, and KRISTELLER, *Philosophy and Rhetoric*, p. 233-234, take a similar view.

[47] MURPHY, *Rhetoric in the Middle Ages*, p. 202-211. Cf. Murphy's earlier essay, *Alberic of Monte Cassino : Father of the Medieval "Ars dictaminis"*, in *American Benedictine Review*, 22 (1971), 129-146. Murphy's view has been supported most recently by Herbert BLOCH, *Monte Cassino's Teachers and Library in the High Middle Ages*, in *La scuola nell'occidente latino dell'alto medioevo* (Settimane di studio del Centro italiano di studi sull'alto medioevo, 19), Spoleto, 1972, p. 593-594, and Robert L. BENSON, *Protohumanism and Narrative Technique in Early Thirteenth-Century Italian 'Ars Dictaminis'*, p. 31-32.

rhetoric of the liberal arts curriculum. He is the earliest known medieval writer on that subject to include letter writing as a major area in which traditional rhetoric might be applied, but his work covers much more that is not strictly relevant to letter writing. The earliest surviving *ars dictandi* and, if Schmale is correct, the composition that actually set out to define the genre, is Adalberto Samaritano's *Praecepta dictaminum*[48]. It would be no more correct to say that Adalberto "invented" the *ars dictaminis* than to say that Alberic did : the tradition was well established before either of them wrote. While Alberic was, so far as is known, the first to write about the rules of letter writing, however, Adalberto was the first to devote an entire treatise to those rules. Moreover, it is from Adalberto's rather than Alberic's work that the textual tradition of the genre, with its distinctive vocabulary, format, and contents, begins. Even Alberic's chief advocate, Hugh of Bologna, owes as much to his rival and contemporary Adalberto as to his predecessor from Monte Cassino.

Before tracing the major developments in the tradition initiated by Adalberto's *Praecepta*, it will be useful to review some of the reasons for the growing interest in letter writing that made it desirable, necessary, perhaps inevitable that an autonomous art of letter writing come into being. The period which produced the earliest *artes dictandi* was one in which political and economic developments increased dramatically the quantity and variety of official documents required by churchmen, the nobility, and private citizens. The stabilization of the feudal domains after centuries of turmoil and the emergence of the first centralized modern states led to an unprecedented volume of diplomatic correspondence, official records, and the like. The Church, as both spiritual and temporal power, was of course directly affected by these same developments and experienced a similar need for new ways to manage demands that overtaxed the old methods. The Investiture Controversy of the late eleventh century was an especially important stimulus to the study of rhetoric as a propaedeutic to the writing of effective propaganda. At least partly due to the increased political stability, the period was equally characterized by economic growth and the expansion of commerce. The

[48] Franz-Josef SCHMALE, *Die Bologneser Schule der 'Ars dictandi'*, in *Deutsches Archiv für Erforschung des Mittelalters*, 13 (1957), 16-34, and Adalbertus SAMARITANUS, *Praecepta dictaminum*, p. 6-11. Others who attack the theory that Alberic "founded" the *ars dictaminis* include PATT and Vincenzo LICITRA, *Il mito del Alberico di Montecassino iniziatore dell' "Ars dictaminis"*, p. 609-627.

intellectual climate of the times was also right for the creation of new disciplines. Europe was experiencing a renewed confidence in the power of human reason to discover and describe the order inherent in nature. Traditional ways of classifying knowledge, like the seven liberal arts, began to be challenged, as did the institutions that perpetuated them. All of these factors are especially evident in northern Italy, where the written tradition of the *ars dictaminis* begins. The emerging city-states of the region, with their self-reliant, often literate bourgeoisie, required a great deal of internal administrative correspondence, as well as correspondence with the neighboring states, the Church, and foreign powers that threatened their independence. Lombardy was an early and famous center of international commerce, while Bologna, with its strong tradition of secular schools, was the site of perhaps the first real university and a center for the study of law, one of the most important of the new disciplines that came into being at the time [49].

The circumstances that fostered the composition of the earliest *artes dictandi* are sharply evident in a persistent debate that was carried on to varying degrees throughout the first major period in the development of the genre. In the second decade of the twelfth century, Adalberto Samaritano, a secular teacher at Bologna, criticized Alberic of Monte Cassino's writings on *dictamen*. The canon Hugh of Bologna, who taught rhetoric at the cathedral school, defended Alberic against these charges in his own *Rationes dictandi* (1119), written very shortly after Adalberto's *Praecepta dictaminum* (1111-1118). The debate between Adalberto and Hugh turned less on specific features of the theory and practice of letter writing than on the context in which the *ars dictaminis* should be taught. A partisan of traditional, ecclesiastical education, Hugh thought the *ars dictaminis* should remain part of and hence subservient to rhetoric in the broader sense ; while Adalberto, a partisan of the newer lay schools, favored the creation of a new discipline, independent of and perhaps in

[49] On the factors that brought about the *ars dictaminis*, see PATT, *Early "Ars dictaminis"* ; Sidney R. HILL, Jr., *"Dictamen" : That Bastard of Literature and Law*, in *The Central States Speech Journal*, 24 (1973), 118-119 ; SCHALLER, *'Ars dictaminis'*, col. 1035, and *Dichtungslehren und Briefsteller*, p. 262-263 ; Martin CAMARGO, *Rhetoric*, in *The Seven Liberal Arts in the Middle Ages*, ed. David WAGNER, Bloomington, 1983, p. 108 ; and WITT, *Medieval Italian Culture and the Origins of Humanism as a Stylistic Ideal.*

time overshadowing the less pragmatic rhetoric of the liberal arts curriculum [50].

Adalberto's position prevailed. The *artes* written by his followers and Hugh's equally numerous followers during the next few decades mark a tradition as distinct from the rhetoric that Alberic taught as were the rising universities from the cathedral schools. And the new discipline's success was such that, for some, rhetoric from the twelfth century on was the *ars dictaminis* [51]. The debate was not entirely resolved, however, and reemerged in a somewhat different form in the early thirteenth century. The cause of this later dispute was the importation of the *ars dictaminis* into France, where it developed certain idiosyncrasies that distinguished it from the Italian variety. The French centers for the study of *dictamen* - Tours, Orléans, Blois, Meung - were also famous centers for studying the classical *auctores*. There, *dictamen* was taught chiefly in conjunction with grammar (indeed, usually by grammar masters), while at Bologna it was associated with the study of law.

The works of the French teachers and the practices of the French notaries who came to work in the papal chancery grew in popularity until they strongly influenced the teaching of *dictamen* at Bologna. Besides adopting such French innovations as the treatment of *cursus*, most early thirteenth-century Italian *dictatores* - for example, Bene da Firenze, Arsegino of Padua, Guido Faba, and even Boncompagno, in his early works - share to some extent the French preoccupation with stylistic ornament and use of the *auctores*. Many of these teachers were, in fact, professors of grammar [52]. However, a reaction against the "French school" of *dictamen* is already evident in Bologna during the first half of the thirteenth century. Sometimes openly, more often implicitly, the Italian *dictatores* took issue with the extensive use of quotations from pagan authors, the unusual or inappropriate vocabulary, and the highly figurative language that characterized French *dictamen*. They advocated instead a simpler, more straightforward style determined by the practical needs of the class of people they trained - chancery clerks, scribes, notaries, etc.

[50] SCHMALE, *Adalbertus*, *Praecepta*, p. 3-4, 9-10 ; MURPHY, *Rhetoric in the Middle Ages*, p. 212-213.

[51] CONSTABLE, *Letters and Letter-Collections*, p. 35 ; WITT, *'Ars Dictaminis' and Humanism*, p. 24.

[52] James R. BANKER, *The "Ars dictaminis" and Rhetorical Textbooks at the Bolognese University in the Fourteenth Century*, in *Medievalia et Humanistica*, n.s. 5 (1974), p. 154.

– rather than by antiquated or purely literary ideals [53]. Thus, while Bene da Firenze defended the use of *auctoritates* and the primacy of verse over prose in his *Summa dictaminis* (before 1216) [54], and included a great deal of "grammatical" material from Matthew of Vendôme, Geoffrey of Vinsauf, and other French sources in his *Candelabrum* (1220-1227), nonetheless in the latter work he carefully distinguished between an Italian approach to *dictamen* and a French one and emphasized the rhetorical nature of *dictamen* to the extent of discussing in some detail all five parts of Ciceronian rhetoric – *inventio, dispositio, elocutio, pronuntiatio,* and *memoria* [55]. Guido Faba includes a catalog of *colores* and a set of proverbs for use as *exordia*, but the simple, clear style of his model letters is in obvious contrast to what is found in the collections of Bernard de Meung. Boncompagno alone, beginning in his *Palma* (1198), attacked directly those who treated *dictamen* as a department of grammar and so undervalued the virtues, such as clarity, proper to prose [56]. By the late thirteenth century the *ars dictaminis* was taught by a newly created professor of rhetoric as part of the regular university curriculum at Bologna [57], and this shift from the connection with grammar entailed a new attention to classical rhetoric that was crucial to the role of the Italian *dictatores* in the rise of humanism. In France and England the association with grammar remained strong throughout the Middle Ages, though the *sermo humilis* of the Italian *dictatores* increasingly displaced the *stilus supremus* of the French school.

If he failed to keep *dictamen* subordinate to the rhetoric of the cathedral schools, Hugh of Bologna is nonetheless distinguished for having established most of what constituted the format of the typical manual of the art. Especially influential was his placement of a group of model letters involving different classes of people, some of them with replies, at the very end of his treatise, following and distinct from the theory. A few

[53] SCHALLER, *Die Kanzlei*, p. 275, 282; MURPHY, *Rhetoric in the Middle Ages*, p. 244; POLAK, *Jacques de Dinant's "Summa dictaminis"*, p. 25-26; WITT, *Boncompagno and the Defense of Rhetoric*, etc.

[54] Paolo MARANGON, *La 'Quadriga' e i 'Proverbi' di maestro Arsegino. Cultura e scuole a Padova prima del 1222*, in *Quaderni per la storia dell' Università di Padova*, 9-10 (1976-1977), 28-31.

[55] Bene does concede that *dictamen* partakes of the other two arts of the *trivium* (I, 4, 5) and he later suggests that it is reducible to *elocutio* (I, 4, 14-16), so he continues to keep one foot in the grammarians' camp.

[56] WITT, *Boncompagno and the Defense of Rhetoric*.

[57] See especially BANKER, *"Ars dictaminis" and Rhetorical Textbooks*.

details of theory, for example the exact number of parts required to make a standard letter, remained to be worked out, but by the mid 1130s the basic form of most subsequent *artes dictandi* had been established.

By the mid twelfth century, the *ars dictaminis* had crossed over to France, by the end of the century it was well established in Germany and had probably reached England, and some time during the thirteenth century it spread to Iberia as well. Only the French, however, seem to have played a major role in the genre's evolution. They adopted the Italian *artes* (Bernard of Bologna's *Summa dictaminum* was especially influential), condensing or expanding as they saw fit, but generally retaining the wording and contents of the theory intact. Their major innovation in the *ars* itself was adding to it a discussion of *cursus*. During the 1180s, the first brief treatment of *cursus* appeared in three dictaminal works of French origin. It is not clear why the *cursus*, which had been observed by the Roman Chancery for centuries, was not made part of the *ars dictaminis* sooner. The French *dictatores* may have added it to their teaching in part because in the late twelfth century some of their students had found employment in Rome. Two of the early versions of the rules for *cursus* refer to the practices of the Roman notaries, and one, attributed (falsely) by the copyist to the papal chancellor and later pope Albert of Morra, is linked in the manuscript to the *Introductiones dictandi* of Transmundus, a French Cistercian who served as papal notary [58]. The addition of *cursus* was an immediate success, and a chapter on the subject became a standard feature of subsequent *artes*.

In addition to the *cursus*, the French also seem to have pioneered the treatment of diplomatics or of specific types of official documents within treatises on *dictamen*. Although already in the late eleventh century Alberic of Monte Cassino devoted a few pages of his *Breviarium de dictamine* to the procedures for drawing up *priuilegia summorum pontificum* and *precepta uel mundiburdia magnarum et secularium potestatum* (ed. ROCKINGER, *Briefsteller*, I, 36-40), and although the notarial art was already being taught at Bologna around the same time, by Irnerius and his successors, the Italian *dictatores* of the twelfth century concentrated almost exclusively on the more literary "missive" letters. As early as the mid twelfth century, however, discussions of the doctrine of privileges

[58] On these early *cursus* texts, see Tore JANSON, *Prose Rhythm*; Ann DALZELL, *The "Forma dictandi" Attributed to Albert of Morra and Related Texts*, in *Mediaeval Studies*, 39 (1977), 440-465; and Martin CAMARGO, *"Libellus" Attributed to Peter of Blois*, p. 19-24.

and legal documents ("*cartae*"), together with substantial collections of model documents, were composed by French *dictatores*, either as separate, brief tracts or as chapters within larger *summae dictandi* such as Bernard de Meung's *Flores dictaminum* [59]. The same sort of "notarial" material is found together with the more "rhetorical" material traditionally associated with the *ars dictaminis* in the works of early thirteenth-century *dictatores* such as Guido Faba and Boncompagno. But by 1221 a separate *ars notariae*, with faculty and textbooks of its own, had arisen in Bologna, and by the early fourteenth century many Italian universities had faculties in the *ars notariae* [60].

In other respects, the theoretical portions of the French treatises were mostly derivative. More original were the collections of model letters or *dictamina* compiled to accompany these schematic *artes*. Transmundus and his contemporary Bernard de Meung produced collections that dwarfed those of their predecessors among the *dictatores*. They intensified the notarial tendency inherent in the *ars dictaminis* from its origins not only by expanding the letter collection but also by incorporating extensive collections of model salutations, *exordia*, and documents. In their works, theory occupied an increasingly small percentage of the whole, and imitation was correspondingly emphasized. Also new was the exploitation of the "literary" possibilities of the model letter collection. Bernard de Meung included a number of letters on fanciful (e.g., mythological) subjects and developed the dramatic potential of the paired letter and response. These developments were continued and extended by the next generation

[59] Charles VULLIEZ chronicles this "pragmatic" orientation of the French *dictatores* in an important study, presented at the XVIe Congrès International des Sciences Historiques (Stuttgart, August 25-September 1, 1985) and forthcoming in *Studi storici*, Rome, Istituto storico italiano per il medio evo : *L'apprentissage de la rédaction des documents diplomatiques à travers l'* "ars dictaminis" *français (et spécialement ligérien) du XII*[e] *siècle*.

[60] The *ars notariae* has been covered briefly in an earlier fascicle (48) in the present series : Guido van DIEVOET, *Les Coutumiers, les Styles, les Formulaires et les "Artes notariae"*, p. 10, 83-84. An excellent short discussion, with full bibliography, is Peter WEIMAR's entry for *ars notariae* in the *Lexikon des Mittelalters*, I : 1045-1047. Harry BRESSLAU, *Handbuch der Urkundenlehre*, II : 256-258, summarizes the contents of the most influential manuals of the *ars notariae*, and James J. MURPHY, *Rhetoric in the Middle Ages*, p. 263-266, discusses the relationship between the *ars notariae* and the *ars dictaminis*. For additional bibliography, see also Murphy's *Medieval Rhetoric : A Select Bibliography*, 2d ed., p. 102-103, and John P. MCGOVERN, *The Documentary Language of Mediaeval Business, A.D. 1150-1250*, in *The Classical Journal*, 67 (1972), 227-239. McGovern emphasizes the distinction between the training and language of "business notaries" and those of the secretarial, letter-writing notaries of chanceries and communes.

of *dictatores*, despite their aversion to certain, mainly stylistic features of the French *dictamina*.

The *ars dictaminis* enters the final phase of its development shortly after 1200, with the rise of a new generation of Italian teachers at Bologna. Many of the features associated with this period in the genre's history were anticipated by the French *dictatores* of the twelfth century, but became more pronounced in the thirteenth century. Large, well-organized collections of model letters and documents like those of Bernard de Meung and Transmundus became the rule, and the format of the *summa dictandi* was firmly established. By the late thirteenth century it was not uncommon for *dictatores* to dispense with theory altogether and to supply nothing but model letters (e.g., Richard of Pofi) or even tables of options from which to assemble a letter (Lawrence of Aquilegia) [61].

Though such treatises resembled the *artes notariae* in their profusion of models and a corresponding paucity of theory, and even, on occasion, in their emphasis on the physical appearance of the document to be produced, nonetheless the *ars dictaminis* and the *ars notariae* remained separate disciplines. The key difference between them is the much stronger association of the *ars notariae* with legal studies : an *ars dictandi* might include chapters covering some of the material treated in an *ars notariae*, but the *artes notariae* ignored the "missive" letters that were the chief concern of the *dictatores*. The commentary found in the *artes notariae*, moreover, was consistently legalistic rather than rhetorical in nature. In Bologna, the prestige of the law faculty was so great that the more legalistic *ars notariae* tended over time to overshadow the related *ars dictaminis*, associated with the arts faculty. In schools where the law was not so dominant, the *ars dictaminis* and the *ars notariae* continued to be taught side by side. In fourteenth- and fifteenth-century Oxford, for example, teachers such as Thomas Sampson and William Kingsmill taught a "business course," one component of which was something very like the *ars notariae*, outside the regular university curriculum ; whereas others, most notably Thomas Merke, composed *artes dictandi* for use within a grammar course supervised by the university's arts faculty.

But this tendency to shift emphasis from the *ars dictaminis* to the *ars notariae* was balanced by the literary preoccupations of many later *dictatores*. Boncompagno, for example, carried the literary potential of the letter collection far beyond the modest limits of Bernard de Meung's

[61] MURPHY, *Rhetoric in the Middle Ages*, p. 261-266.

experiment by composing complex narratives involving sequences of seven or more letters [62]. And though they did not ornament their model letters with classical allusions to the same extent as the French *dictatores*, many of the thirteenth-century Italian teachers studied the *auctores* in connection with *dictamen* and took Cicero as their stylistic model [63].

Moreover, not all *dictatores*, neither in Italy nor in France, participated in the shift from *theoria* to *practica*. Alongside the collections of genuine or fabricated models for imitation by men such as Pier della Vigna, Thomas of Capua, Berard of Naples, and Richard of Pofi, are treatises that consist mainly of theory, supplemented with relatively few illustrative models. Bene da Firenze, whose *Candelabrum* is the most comprehensive treatise of the latter sort, criticized those who taught the art of the salutation solely through formulae or models. They know only the semblances (*simulacra*) of the art and not its principle (*doctrina*), and their teaching is more appropriate for rustics than for educated people (III, 56) [64]. Even more outspoken on this topic was Jean de Limoges, who set out in his *Libellus de dictamine et dictatorio syllogismorum* (late twelfth or early thirteenth century) to make the *ars dictaminis* more systematic by assimilating it to the more universal art of dialectic, which, allied with theology, ruled the university of Paris. He attributed the widespread disagreement about the rules of *dictamen* and the consequent decline in the quality of its practice to his contemporaries' neglect of the fixed principles or precepts of the art. Those who do not ground the *ars dictaminis* firmly in the "places" or the principles of invention but rather in the multiplicity of letters and *clausulae*, he says, are like those who, wishing to provide a way to prevent foot pain, skip over the lessons of the shoemaker's art and simply display diverse pairs of shoes [65]. Some *dictatores* – Lawrence of Aquilegia, for example – wrote both a theoretical treatise and a separate treatise relying almost exclusively on models, perhaps in order to attract the broadest possible range of students.

[62] BENSON, *Protohumanism and Narrative Technique*, p. 40-50. Also see Boncompagno, *Rota Veneris*, ed. and trans. Josef PURKART, Delmar, N.Y., 1975.

[63] Helene WIERUSZOWSKI, *Rhetoric and the Classics in Italian Education of the Thirteenth Century*, in *Studia Gratiana*, 11 (1967), 169-208 ; POLAK, *Jacques de Dinant's "Summa dictaminis"*, p. 26-31 *et passim* ; KRISTELLER, *Philosophy and Rhetoric*, p. 239 ; BENSON, *Protohumanism and Narrative Technique*, p. 39-40.

[64] Ed. Gian Carlo ALESSIO, *Bene Florentini Candelabrum* (Thesaurus Mundi, 23), Padua, 1983, p. 128.

[65] Ed. Constantin HORVATH, *Johannis Lemovicensis, Abbatis de Zirc 1208-1218. Opera omnia*, Veszprem, 1932, vol. 1, p. 4.

Giovanni di Bonandrea and his successors cast an even wider net : they taught the *Rhetorica ad Herennium* to students at the university of Bologna but the *ars dictaminis* to the municipal notaries [66]. Though the rivalry between the "notarial" and the "arts course" approaches to teaching *dictamen* became less explicit as time went on, the competing approaches can still be observed, for example in Oxford, as late as the fifteenth century.

Where the later Italian *dictatores* differed most sharply from their twelfth-century predecessors was in their sense of their own prestige and that of their discipline and in their corresponding expansion of the scope of their concerns [67]. Both developments were probably due in part to the elevation of the *ars dictaminis* to a distinct field of study, with its own faculty, at Bologna [68], and in part to the more prominent civic role played by each successive generation of *dictatores*. In terms of the works written, this new sense of prestige produced what appear to be opposite tendencies. On the one hand, there were large treatises, such as Bene da Firenze's *Candelabrum* and Boncompagno's *Rhetorica antiqua*, that are more systematic and comprehensive than anything that preceded them. On the other hand, there is a proliferation of short, highly specialized manuals dealing with a single type of document or a single part of a letter, many of them written by the same men who wrote the larger *summae* (e.g., Boncompagno, Guido Faba, Matteo dei Libri, Lawrence of Aquilegia, Jacques de Dinant). These shorter treatises may, however, reflect the new status of the *ars dictaminis* if in fact they were designed to permit students to take a series of courses in the subject, each with a fairly high degree of technical detail. Perhaps the brief tracts were also composed to supplement existing works or to permit flexibility in organizing courses on the *ars dictaminis*, since they rarely appeared in isolation but were typically copied together with related works by the same or another author to form a comprehensive collection. The topic merits further study.

Many of them were practising notaries who, along with the lawyers, played a key role in carrying on the business and government of the communes and in articulating the aspirations of the rising class that

[66] See BANKER, *"Ars dictaminis" and Rhetorical Textbooks*, p. 157-163.

[67] BENSON, *Protohumanism and Narrative Technique*, p. 34-38.

[68] See especially Augusto GAUDENZI, *Sulla cronologia delle opere dei dettatori bolognesi da Buoncompagno a Bene di Lucca*, in *Bullettino dell'Istituto storico italiano*, 14 (1895), 85-174, and Giuseppe VECCHI, *Il magistero delle "Artes" Latine a Bologna nel medioevo* (Publicazioni della Facoltà di Magistero, Università di Bologna, 2), Bologna, 1958.

came to dominate those communes. Though many of the northern *dictatores* also practised their art outside the schools (Transmundus, for example, was a prominent papal notary during the 1180s), they did not operate within the civic context that forged such a vital link between the learning and the political activity of the Italian *dictatores*, especially from the middle of the thirteenth century on. Over time, those *dictatores* tied their ambitions to those of the class they served, becoming spokesmen for a secularism that ultimately sought its validation in the literature of classical antiquity. One sign of this civic involvement is the melding of the *ars dictaminis* and the *Rhetorica ad Herennium*, by thirteenth-century *dictatores* such as Boncompagno, Guido Faba, and Matteo dei Libri, to create a medieval art of composing public speeches in Latin or Italian (*ars arengandi*), which they taught along with their other subjects [69]. From the existence of these *artes arengandi*, together with collections of model speeches for use by public officials and copies of speeches actually delivered, P.O. Kristeller concludes "that in Italy, in the thirteenth and perhaps even in the twelfth century, all genres of secular speech that were to be cultivated by the Renaissance humanists had come into being out of the legal, political, and social institutions of the later Middle Ages, and that they were composed in the rhetorical style of the time, that of the *dictatores*, long before the humanists had a chance to apply to them their own different standards of style." A harbinger of the revival of a fully Ciceronian rhetoric, this facet of the later *dictatores*' activities, like their self-awareness, their literary preoccupations, and their cultivation of a clear, straightforward style, marks them as forerunners of the humanists [70].

A final characteristic of the later *dictatores*, the composition of models

[69] KRISTELLER, *Philosophy and Rhetoric*, p. 237-238, 320-321. See also Carlo FRATI, *"Flore de parlare" o "Somma d'arengare" attribuita a Ser Giovanni Fiorentino da Vignano in un codice Marciano*, in *Giornale storico della letteratura italiana*, 61 (1913), 1-31, 228-265, and André WILMART, *"L'Ars arengandi " de Jacques de Dinant avec un Appendice sur ses ouvrages "De dictamine"*, in *Analecta Reginensia* (Studi e Testi, 59), Vatican City, 1933, p. 113-151. Helene WIERUSZOWSKI discusses the civic role of the *dictatores* in several of the essays collected in *Politics and Culture in Medieval Spain and Italy* (Storia e letteratura, Raccolta di studi e testi, 121), Rome, 1971, pt. II.

[70] KRISTELLER, *Philosophy and Rhetoric*, p. 238. Kristeller first advanced his thesis in *Humanism and Scholasticism in the Italian Renaissance*, in *Byzantion*, 17 (1944-1945), 346-374. See also Jerrold E. SEIGEL, *Rhetoric and Philosophy in Renaissance Humanism : The Union of Eloquence and Wisdom, Petrarch to Valla*, Princeton, 1968, p. 200-225 ; Lauro MARTINES, *Power and Imagination : City-States in Renaissance Italy*, New York, 1979, p. 201-207 ; and WITT, *"Ars Dictaminis" and Humanism.*

and occasionally entire treatises in the vernacular, also had its beginning in the thirteenth century. Examples include the bilingual *Parlamenta et Epistole* (1242-1243) and *Gemma purpurea* of Guido Faba [71], the Italian *Dicerie* of Matteo dei Libri [72], Book Three of Brunetto Latini's French *Trésor* [73], and the same author's Italian *Rettorica* (after 1260) and *Sommetta* (c. 1275) [74]. Use of the vernacular in dictaminal writings was rare outside Italy during the thirteenth century but became more common in the fourteenth and fifteenth centuries [75].

The fourteenth- and fifteenth-century treatises have not been studied as carefully as the earlier ones, but they seem in general to repeat the doctrine of the thirteenth-century *dictatores*, while adapting their models to the time and place of their intended use. The reliance on models for copying reached its most extreme form during this period in works such as Lawrence of Aquilegia's very popular *Practica sive usus dictaminis*, but the conventional *summae dictandi*, with their mixture of theory and example, continued to be produced through the fifteenth century (and beyond). There appears to have been an increased tendency to create compendia out of extracts from several *artes* and to blend theoretical commentary into the letter collection in the form of a commentary or running gloss, but much more study of the unpublished materials will be necessary before it is possible to generalize about such phenomena. What is fairly certain is that few significant innovations in the contents of dictaminal manuals occurred after the thirteenth century. The century that marked the height of the *ars dictaminis*' popularity and prestige also saw the end of its creative evolution.

[71] See Arrigo CASTELLANI, *Le formule volgari di Guido Faba*, p. 5-78, and Augusto GAUDENZI, *I suoni, le forme e le parole dell'odierno dialetto della città di Bologna*, Turin, 1889, p. 127-160.

[72] See KRISTELLER, *Matteo de'Libri*, p. 284-285.

[73] Ed. Francis J. CARMODY, *Li Livres dou Tresor* (University of California Publications in Modern Philology, 22), Berkeley, 1948, p. 317-422. Also see James R. EAST, *Book Three of Brunetto Latini's "Tresor" : An English Translation and Assessment of Its Contribution to Rhetorical Theory* (Diss. Stanford 1960) and *Brunetto Latini's Rhetoric of Letter Writing*, in *The Quarterly Journal of Speech*, 54 (1968), 241-246.

[74] SCHALLER, *"Ars dictaminis"*, col. 1036.

[75] *Ibid.*, cols. 1037-1038. For bilingual *artes dictandi* in fourteenth- and fifteenth-century England, see Martin CAMARGO, *The Middle English Love Letter and Its Rhetorical Background* (Diss. Illinois 1978), p. 23-32.

CHAPTER III

RULES OF CRITICISM

In using dictaminal materials as sources for historical study, one must be constantly aware of the means by which such materials were transmitted and the context in which they were employed. Unfortunately, it is precisely in these areas where the most research remains to be done. Some gaps in the chain of transmission will never be filled because treatises have been lost or because the oral teaching of the important *dictatores* was never written in an organized and comprehensive form. But a great deal is still to be learned from the many manuscripts that survive, very few of which, relatively speaking, have been studied in the detail that they require. The fact that fewer than half of the extant *artes dictandi* have been printed poses logistical obstacles for those concerned with problems of transmission, and of course the complex and unresolved problems of transmission discourage in turn many a would-be editor. Moreover, manuscripts containing relevant material are to be found in nearly every major library in Europe (and many in America as well) and are frequently catalogued so vaguely or incorrectly that they escape the notice of even very careful researchers. This last obstacle should become far less daunting once Emil Polak's census of dictaminal manuscripts in European libraries has been completed.

Those textual studies that have already been written indicate at least some of the problems that concern prospective users of dictaminal writings. On Adalberto Samaritano and his followers, see Ernst H. KANTOROWICZ, *Anonymi "Aurea Gemma"*, in *Medievalia et Humanistica*, 1 (1943), 41-57, and Franz-Josef SCHMALE, *Die Bologneser Schule der "Ars Dictandi "*, in *Deutsches Archiv für Erforschung des Mittelalters*, 13 (1957), 16-34 ; on Bernard of Bologna, Charles H. HASKINS, *An Italian Master Bernard*, in *Essays in History Presented to Reginald Lane POOLE*, ed. Henry W.C. DAVIS, Oxford, 1927, p. 211-226. Bernard de Meung has been the subject of numerous textual studies, most recently CAMARGO, *The English Manuscripts of Bernard of Meung's "Flores Dictaminum"*, p. 197-219, and VULLIEZ, *Un nouveau manuscrit 'parisien' de la "Summa dictaminis" de Bernard de Meung et sa place dans la tradition manuscrite du texte*, p. 133-151. For another late twelfth-century work, see CAMARGO,

The "Libellus de arte dictandi rhetorice" Attributed to Peter of Blois, p. 16-41. Fewer studies have been done of the later texts, which tend to survive in greater numbers, but see especially Ernst H. KANTOROWICZ, *Petrus de Vinea in England*, in *Mitteilungen des österreichischen Instituts für Geschichtsforschung*, 51 (1937), 43-88, and *An 'Autobiography' of Guido Faba*, in *Mediaeval and Renaissance Studies*, 1 (1941-1943), 253-280 ; and Gian Carlo ALESSIO, *La tradizione manoscritta del "Candelabrum" di Bene da Firenze*, in *Italia medioevale e umanistica*, 15 (1972), 99-148. The introductions to the best modern editions of *artes dictandi* also contain information on transmission and dissemination.

The chief problem, that of distinguishing authentic from fabricated letters, has been discussed by many scholars, but especially well by Constable [76]. Although the issue of authenticity is limited to the collections of model letters and documents, it has generally been that component of the *summae dictandi*, rather than the theory, that historians have found most valuable. Whether they occur separately or accompanied by a theoretical *ars dictandi*, these "didactic letter collections" must be approached with all of the caution recommended by Constable and others. The *dictatores* could and did produce letters and documents that looked deceptively like the real thing but were in fact only loosely based on genuine documents or completely fabricated. In some cases they incorporated actual documents into their collections, though rarely without altering names, places, and other details as befit the circumstances of their use. As such collections were disseminated throughout Europe, subsequent adapters performed the same operation. A letter by a master at Bologna, for example, might be copied *verbatim* in the model collection of a different *dictator* and appear a generation later as the work of a Parisian master, whence later still as that of an Oxford *dictator*. Such changes are less common as a given letter's contents are more circumstantial ; but circumstantial details could also be changed in the course of transmission.

Whether their models were pure fictions, adaptations of genuine letters, or authentic documents (a single collection might contain examples of all three types), the *dictatores* were always concerned less with factual accuracy than with stylistic correctness and pedagogical effectiveness.

[76] *Letters and Letter-Collections*, p. 42-62. Also see SCHALLER, *Dichtungslehren und Briefsteller*, p. 262.

They did not hesitate to tamper with the wording of authentic documents, even if such tampering altered the factual content, if they felt that they could thereby cause the texts they selected to fit their stylistic precepts more neatly [77]. As teachers, the *dictatores* naturally chose documents that would interest their students as well as illustrate their teaching. By the same token, when composing fictional models they were apt to allude to those persons and events most familiar and most interesting to their students. In so doing, however, they were not constrained to produce faithful accounts, but might use the occasion for idealizing, for moralizing, or simply for playing to the galleries. If one took Bernard de Meung's collection at face value, for example, one would be compelled to conclude that sex crimes were so widespread among the twelfth-century clergy that bishops had time for little else besides combatting them. The comic and sensational were as appealing to medieval as to modern students, and the *dictatores* were not averse to exploiting that appeal.

A good rule is to presume that some tampering has occurred whenever dealing with a letter or document that is part of a didactic collection. The text in question may well prove to be genuine, but it must be presumed guilty until positive evidence can be cited to the contrary. The problem then becomes that of determining whether a given letter or collection was composed or compiled for didactic purposes. This task is simplest when the collection is well established as the work of a known teacher and is preserved in several manuscripts containing his work. Even in such a case, however, one must beware of interpolations – just as the fictional letters of Bernard de Meung were occasionally passed off as authentic letters of Peter of Blois, so too genuine letters found their way into manuscripts whose contents were otherwise fictional. Even letter collections composed to accompany specific *artes dictandi* often ended up circulating independently, undergoing in the process frequent changes of content and even format. A collection that occurs in a manuscript containing mainly works on law and rhetoric or, in northern Europe, on grammar and other school subjects was at least thought to be didactic by the scribe who prepared the manuscript. If the collection is also divided in the characteristic manner, that is, by subject or by the social status of the recipients, then the presumption of didactic intent is

[77] For a good example, see I.S. ROBINSON, *The 'Colores Rhetorici' in the Investiture Contest*, in *Traditio*, 32 (1976), 209-238.

strengthened. But the absence of such corroborating evidence does not necessarily disprove such intent.

Also of use in distinguishing didactic from other sorts of letters and letter collections are stylistic considerations. Very strict observance of the *cursus*, regular use of proverbs at the beginning of letters, brevity that verges on superficiality within the body of a letter, the recurrence of the same formulas of greeting and farewell, and very sharp articulation of the five-part schema are among the chief signs that can help to confirm a collection's dictaminal quality. Such evidence must be used cautiously, especially when applied to a single letter, because the *ars dictaminis* established the stylistic canons that guided most official letter writers during the later Middle Ages. From the late twelfth century on, most genuine letters, even those by acknowledged master stylists such as Pier della Vigna, show the influence of the *ars dictaminis*, and many are just as slavish in their adherence to its rules as are the models used in teaching those rules [78].

The practice of spurious attribution mentioned above is one aspect of a second major problem, one that affects the theoretical *artes* as well as the collections of models. Because the *ars dictaminis* was so fundamentally pragmatic a discipline, its practitioners never hesitated to adapt their material as the needs of the moment demanded. One frequently encounters compendia that draw on a number of different treatises and that must have been compiled *ad hoc*. In some cases the compiler supplies a prologue wherein he identifies at least some of his sources [79], but frequently there is no indication that the treatise is anything but an "original" composition [80]. To distinguish between an "original" *ars dictandi* and a "mere" compendium is admittedly difficult, since the conventional doctrine and vocabulary of the *dictatores* became fixed at so early a point in the history of the genre. The same authorities were cited from treatise to treatise with such regularity that direct borrowing is difficult to determine unless verbal parallels are extremely close and external evidence is available to corroborate the hypothesis. So prevalent was the adaptation,

[78] See, for example, CONSTABLE, *Letters and Letter-Collections*, p. 36-38.

[79] See CAMARGO, *"Libellus" Attributed to Peter of Blois*, p. 18-19.

[80] Such compilers have at times misled cataloguers by using a well-known *incipit*. For an example, see CAMARGO, *The English Manuscripts of Bernard of Meung's "Flores dictaminum"*, in *Viator*, 12 (1981), 213-214.

interpolation, abbreviation, and expansion of such material that it can be extremely difficult, perhaps impossible, to establish the definitive text even of so important a work as Bernard de Meung's *Flores dictaminum* [81].

[81] Of Bernard, Hans Martin SCHALLER has said : "Kein anderer Lehrer des Ars dictandi hat eine so grosse Wirkung auf Mit- und Nachwelt ausgeübt..." (*Lexikon des Mittelalters*, 1, col. 2001).

CHAPTER IV

DISSEMINATION

Just as a work's identity can become obscured as it is copied and recopied, so can the lines of its influence on other works. Selective borrowings are difficult to trace when they could have come from one of several sources or when names and other details have been changed to fit another time and place. Subsequent writers were seldom content to copy their source, except for brief excerpts. More typically they retained the basic wording of a passage but expanded, abbreviated, or embellished it at will. Historically, the tendency was to mix material from one treatise with that from another, especially one considered more authoritative on a given point than the chief source. The result was the *vel ... vel ...* construction that typifies the *artes dictandi*, particularly the sections treating basic definitions and the variations possible within the *salutatio*. From this legitimate desire to juxtapose authorities, the later *compendia* apparently evolved.

Within Italy, the integrity of individual treatises seems to have been better maintained than elsewhere. If this impression is correct, the explanation has probably to do with the greater prestige of the *ars dictaminis* and the better defined context for its teaching and use. The faculty of *dictamen* at Bologna has already been mentioned, as has the increasingly important role of the *dictator* in the civic life of the Italian communes. Also important is the role of the Roman Curia, whose notaries produced a number of important dictaminal treatises (especially collections of didactic models) beginning in the late twelfth century [82]. Outside Italy, teachers tended to adapt the theory of the recognized experts, especially the Italian Guido Faba, and to exercise their imaginations, if at all, on the model documents. In France and England, moreover, the *ars dictaminis* came to occupy a very ambiguous position in the school *curricula*, where it was taught in association with grammar. Whereas little is known as yet about the details of such instruction, its results are clear not only in the "pagan" style of the French *dictatores* but also in the fact that among

[82] BRESSLAU, *Handbuch der Urkundenlehre*, p. 264-268 ; SCHALLER, *"Ars dictaminis"*, col. 1037.

French and English writers discussions of *dictamen* often occur within treatises that deal chiefly with poetry [83], that English *dictatores* sometimes borrow extensively from English *versificatores* in their teaching (the chief sources of Thomas Merke's treatise, for example, are Geoffrey of Vinsauf's *Poetria nova* and *Documentum*), and that in English and French manuscripts *artes dictandi* very commonly occur in the company of *artes versificandi* and other grammatical materials.

With so relatively vague a concept of the discipline's boundaries, it is not surprising that instruction focused more on the use of letter collections as primary texts into which brief theoretical observations were inserted almost as glosses. It is no wonder that Lawrence of Aquilegia's schematic *Practica* was more popular than his more conventionally organized *Speculum dictaminis*. In fact, a thorough textual history of that very popular early fourteenth-century work, which occurs in very different forms in the many manuscripts that preserve it and which is not even consistently attributed to Lawrence, would illuminate much that remains obscure about the transmission and use of dictaminal doctrine during the later Middle Ages. Such study of Bernard de Meung's work has already begun to yield important insights, particularly into the role of the *ars dictaminis* in Germany. Similar results could be expected from studying the dissemination of the writings of Guido Faba, one of the most prolific and, along with Bernard de Meung, the most influential of the *dictatores*.

As a rule, the more space a given *ars dictandi* devoted to theory (as opposed to models) the more likely the integrity of its text would be preserved in the course of transmission. Also influencing textual integrity was the authority a treatise achieved. The "definitive editions" of Guido Faba's *Summa dictaminis* and Thomas of Capua's *Ars dictandi*, each surviving in 50 or more copies [84], remained intact through nearly two

[83] See GEOFFREY OF VINSAUF, *Documentum de modo et arte dictandi et versificandi* (commonly called 'Tria Sunt'); GERVASE OF MELKLEY, *Ars versificaria*; and JOHN OF GARLAND, *De arte prosayca, metrica, et rithmica* or *Poetria Parisiana*. Geoffrey may also have written a *summa dictandi* during a stay at Bologna. See Vincenzo LICITRA, *La "Summa de arte dictandi" di Maestro Goffredo*, in *Studi medievali*, ser. 3, 7 (1966), 865-913.

[84] Charles FAULHABER gives references for 41 mss. of Guido's work, indicating that the list is certainly incomplete: *The "Summa dictaminis" of Guido Faba*, in *Medieval Eloquence : Studies in the Theory and Practice of Medieval Rhetoric*, ed. James J. MURPHY, Berkeley and Los Angeles, 1978, p. 86 n. 2. Emmy HELLER knew of 48 mss. of Thomas' work: *Die Ars dictandi des Thomas von Capua* (Sitzungsberichte der Heidelberger Akademie der

centuries of use throughout Europe. Other treatises were more narrowly restricted in their authority to a particular time and place, where they enjoyed the status of standard *curriculum* text. Good examples are Giovanni di Bonandrea's *Brevis introductio ad dictamen*, in fourteenth-century Bologna, and Thomas Merke's *Formula moderni et usitati dictaminis*, in fifteenth-century Oxford.

Some of the standard school texts acquired glosses or commentaries in the course of their use. Most of the surviving copies of Giovanni di Bonandrea's treatise contain some form of commentary, for example, and John of Vienna's *Exposicio super summa dictaminum Ludolfi de Hildeshemio* is found in two Czechoslovakian manuscripts [85]. However, teachers were more likely to develop a separate, if highly derivative text rather than a commentary, in the process changing names, places, and even minor details of fact ; borrowing supplementary material from other works or adding models of their own devising ; and omitting those portions that they considered irrelevant, outmoded, or obscure. Though often these later redactors announced their intentions, just as often they supplied no clue as to what they had done with their source. As the distance separating the redactor from the initial composer of the work becomes greater, the likelihood that all of the modifications just described will occur increases correspondingly, as does the degree to which the resulting text will diverge from its source. When one considers that the last surge of innovative *artes* came during the first half of the thirteenth century, it is easy to imagine how thoroughly the traditions of the major texts had interpenetrated by the fifteenth century, when men such as Valla and Erasmus began to replace them with *artes epistolandi* that took Cicero's prose for their model of style.

The dissemination process can be illustrated particularly well by tracing the history of Bernard of Bologna's *Summa dictaminum*. Itself a revision and expansion of the anonymous Bolognese *Rationes dictandi* (c. 1135), Bernard's treatise was first composed in 1144 or 1145 and then revised by the author between 1145 and 1153. The second redaction is found north of the Alps by 1160, where the names of persons and places are

Wissenschaften, Philosophisch-historische Klasse, Jahrgang 1928/29, 4. Abhandlung), Heidelberg, 1929, p. 5.

[85] Emil Polak informed me of this commentary, extant in mss. from Prague and Vyšší Brod. On glossed copies of Giovanni di Bonandrea's work, see BANKER, *"Ars dictaminis" and Rhetorical Textbooks*, p. 160-162. One of the 18 mss. of Bene da Firenze's *Candelabrum* is glossed : ALESSIO, *Bene Florentini Candelabrum*, p. XLIX.

changed in the models and where some new material, for example a treatise on privileges, is added [86]. This northern version was by turns condensed, excerpted, and interpolated to produce such "new" works as the *Libellus de arte dictandi rhetorice* (1181-1185) attributed in the unique manuscript to Peter of Blois (Cambridge University Library, MS Dd.9.38, fols. 115ra-121ra) ; the anonymous *Ars dictandi aurelianensis* (1180s) printed by Rockinger (*Briefsteller*, I : 103-114) ; the *ars dictandi* that was the first part of Bernard de Meung's *Flores dictaminum* (various versions, from the 1180s and 1190s) ; and the *Summa dictaminis Magistri Bernardi* (late twelfth century) ascribed by its editor to Bernard Silvestris [87]. Through the works of Bernard de Meung, of which nearly 40 manuscript copies are known, Bernard of Bologna's influence continued to be felt throughout Europe as late as the fifteenth century. Of course, Bernard de Meung's work underwent the same processes of excerpting, interpolation, and "refining" as his predecessor's did, and so with the passage of time the lines of influence became increasingly blurred. Similar, though perhaps less complex illustrations of the dissemination process could be given for other major authorities through careful attention to the many *compendia* that survive from the twelfth through the fifteenth centuries. My own research on English *compendia* of the late fourteenth and early fifteenth centuries, for example, shows that along with Bernard de Meung, Guido Faba and Thomas of Capua were still being quoted (if not always acknowledged) two centuries after they wrote.

[86] HASKINS, *Italian Master Bernard*, p. 211-226. I have also relied on unpublished material by Richard Spence, who is preparing a critical edition of Bernard's treatise.

[87] Mirella BRINI SAVORELLI, *Il 'dictamen' di Bernardo Silvestre*, in *Rivista critica di storia della filosofia*, 20 (1965), 182-230.

CHAPTER V

EDITIONS

Though a good many *artes dictandi* have been printed, many more remain in manuscript. A large proportion of those printed, moreover, are in need of new, modern editions. The essential collection of primary material is Ludwig Rockinger's *Briefsteller und Formelbücher des eilften bis vierzehnten Jahrhunderts* (2 vols. ; 1863-1864), which brings together full or partial texts of eighteen different works spanning virtually the entire history of the *ars dictaminis* and representing all the regions in Western Europe where it was cultivated. Now well over a century old, Rockinger's collection must be used with some caution. The partial editions can be misleading. For example, Rockinger prints only the parts of Alberic of Monte Cassino's *Breviarium de dictamine* that deal with letter writing, while the treatise as a whole covers a much wider range of material [88]. Also, the commentary is dated and sometimes erroneous, as when Rockinger attributes the anonymous Bolognese *Rationes dictandi* (c. 1135) to Alberic of Monte Cassino. And the editions are based on fewer, often less authoritative manuscripts than are now known. His edition of Konrad von Mure (II : 417-482) has now been superseded by Walter Kronbichler (ed.), *Die Summa de arte prosandi des Konrad von Mure*, Geist und Werk der Zeiten, Heft 17 (Zurich, 1968). John of Garland's treatise, from which Rockinger published extracts (II : 490-512), has since been edited by Giovanni Mari, "Poetria magistri Johannis Anglici de arte prosayca metrica et rithmica", *Romanische Forschungen*, 13 (1902), 883-965 (excluding the *ars rhythmica*, which he published in *I trattati medievali di ritmica latina* [Milan, 1899], p. 35-80), and Traugott Lawler (ed. and trans.), *The Parisiana Poetria of John of Garland*, Yale Studies in English, 182 (New Haven, 1974). But even with its limitations, Rockinger's collection offers a fairly representative sampling of the materials that constituted the *ars dictaminis* (albeit with disproportionate

[88] The entire *Breviarium* has been edited by Peter-Christian GROLL, in Part 2 of his doctoral dissertation : *Das "Enchiridion de prosis et de rithmis" des Alberich von Montecassino und die Anonymi "ars dictandi"*, Freiburg im Breisgau, 1963.

attention to German authors) and the only printed editions of several important treatises.

Several of the most significant texts have been printed only in brief extracts, Bernard de Meung's *Flores dictaminum* and Boncompagno's masterwork, the *Rhetorica antiqua* or *Boncompagnus* being the most notable examples. Among those who have printed extracts from Bernard de Meung's work are Lucien Auvray, "Documents orléanais du xiie et du xiiie siècle : Extraits du formulaire de Bernard de Meung", *Extraits des Mémoires de la Société archéologique et historique de l'Orléanais*, 23 (1892), 393-415 ; Oswald Redlich, "Eine Wiener Briefsammlung zur Geschichte des deutschen Reiches und der österreichischen Länder in der zweiten Hälfte des XIII. Jahrhunderts", *Mittheilungen aus dem vatikanischen Archive*, 2 (Vienna, 1894), 336-367 ; Alexander Cartellieri, *Ein Donaueschingen Briefsteller : Lateinische Stilübungen des XII. Jahrhunderts aus der Orléans'schen Schule* (Innsbruck, 1898) ; and Léopold Delisle, "Notice sur une 'Summa dictaminis' jadis conservée à Beauvais", *Notices et extraits*, 36 (1899), 171-201. Though only selections from the *Rhetorica antiqua* have been printed (e.g., by Rockinger, *Briefsteller*, I : 128-174), several of Boncompagno's briefer works have received full editions : *Cedrus*, ed. Rockinger, *Briefsteller*, I : 121-127 ; *Rhetorica novissima*, ed. Augusto Gaudenzi, in *Bibliotheca iuridica medii aevi*, 2 (Bologna, 1892), 249-297 ; *Palma*, ed. Carl Sutter, *Aus Leben und Schriften des Magisters Boncompagno* (Freiburg im Breisgau, 1894), p. 105-127. His *Rota Veneris* has been edited three times, most recently in facsimile (of the incunabulum) by Josef Purkart (Delmar, N.Y., 1975), and a critical edition is currently being prepared by Giuseppe Vecchi.

Most of Guido Faba's eight major works have been printed, but only one of them – the *Summa de vitiis et virtutibus* – in a satisfactory edition [89]. Giovanni di Bonandrea's influential *Summa dictaminis* or *Brevis introductio ad dictamen* has been edited by James R. Banker, as Appendix A (p. 329ff) to his doctoral dissertation [90]. A few extracts from the *Brevis introductio* were also printed by Guido Zaccagnini, in "Giovanni di Bonandrea dettatore e rimatore e altri grammatici e dottori in arti dello studio bolognese", *Studi e memorie per la storia dell'Università di Bologna*,

[89] For bibliography, see FAULHABER, *"Summa" of Guido Faba*, p. 87-90. Faulhaber emphasizes the need for a new edition of the *Summa dictaminis*.

[90] See Bibliography above. For the importance of Giovanni di Bonandrea, see especially BANKER, *"Ars dictaminis" and Rhetorical Textbooks*.

5 (1920), 147-204, and an anonymous translation of the same work into Italian (second half of the fourteenth century) was published over a century ago by Francesco Zambrini : *Giovanni Bonandrea, Brieve introductione a dictare* (Bologna, 1854). Lawrence of Aquilegia, whose works were widely used throughout Europe from the fourteenth century on, has not fared as well. His most popular textbook, the *Practica sive usus dictaminis*, has been edited twice, both times from single manuscripts : Rockinger, *Briefsteller*, II : 956-966, and Sanç Capdevila, "La 'Practica dictaminis' de Lorens de Aquilegia en un codex de Tarragona", *Analecta Sacra Tarraconensia*, 6 (1930), 210-229. Though F. Novati edited a portion of the *Summa dictaminis* nearly a century ago, in *L'influsso del pensiero latino sulla civiltà italiana del Medio Evo* (Milan, 1889), p. 251-254, Lawrence's other writings have received little scholarly attention and remain in manuscript.

Editions of several other important works, such as Adalberto Samaritano's *Praecepta dictaminum* and Alberic of Monte Cassino's *Dictaminum radii*, have been noted earlier in the essay, and James J. Murphy's *Medieval Rhetoric : A Select Bibliography* can be consulted for editions of some of the less important ones (see especially p. 59-64 and 67-69). Among the editions that were omitted from Murphy's list or have appeared since its publication are Botho Odebrecht, "Die Briefmuster des Henricus Francigena", *Archiv für Urkundenforschung*, 14 (1936), 231-261 (partial edition of *Aurea Gemma* : letters only) ; Vito Sivo, "Le *Introductiones Dictandi* di Paolo Camaldolese (Testo inedito del sec. XII ex.)", *Studi e ricerche dell'Istituto di Latino*, vol. 3 (Genoa, 1980), 69-100 ; Giuseppe Vecchi, *Magistri Boni Lucensis Cedrus Libani*, Testi e manuali del Istituto di filologia romanza dell'Università di Roma, 46 (Modena, 1963) ; Vincenzo Licitra, "La *Summa de arte dictandi* di Maestro Goffredo", *Studi medievali*, ser. 3, 7 (1966), 865-913 ; Valeria Bertolucci Pizzorusso, "Un trattato di *ars dictandi* dedicato ad Alfonso X", *Studi mediolatini e volgari*, 15-16 (1968), 9-88 (partial edition of Geoffrey of Everseley, *Ars epistolaris ornatus* ; full edition in progress) ; Sándor Durzsa, "Il *Liber dictaminum* di Baldwinus", *Quadrivium*, 13, 2 (1972), 5-41 ; Emil J. Polak, *A Textual Study of Jacques de Dinant's Summa dictaminis*, Études de philologie et d'histoire, 28 (Geneva, 1975) ; Charles B. Faulhaber, *Juan Gil de Zamora, Dictaminis epithalamium*, Biblioteca degli Studi mediolatini e volgari, n.s. 2 (Pisa, 1978) ; Vincenzo Licitra, *Il Pomerium rethorice di Bichilino da Spello* (Florence, 1979) ; and David Thomson and James J. Murphy, "Dictamen as a Developed Genre : The Fourteenth-Century 'Brevis doctrina dictaminis' of Ventura da Bergamo", *Studi medievali*, ser. 3, 23 (1982), 361-386. The *Summa dictaminis* and *Epistolarium* by Pons de Provence have been edited, as part of a thesis, by Henri-Georges Le Saulnier de Saint-Jouan : "Pons le Provencal, maitre en 'Dictamen' (XIIIe siècle)", 2 vols., typed (Paris, 1957). A résumé can be found in the *Positions* of theses at the École des Chartes for 1957 (p. 87-92).

A great deal of recent and current research has been devoted to producing critical editions of the *artes dictandi*. Gian Carlo Alessio's imposing edition of Bene da Firenze's *Candelabrum* is a notable product of this work : *Bene Florentini Candelabrum*, Thesaurus Mundi, 23 (Padua, 1983). Alessio also plans a history of the *ars dictaminis* in Italy, with abundant extracts from the primary texts (on the model of Charles Thurot's study of medieval grammar). Among the other editorial projects under way are Bernard of Bologna, *Summa dictaminum* (by Richard Spence)[91] ; Henricus Francigena, *Aurea Gemma* and Ralph of Vendôme (?), *Cognito* (by Charles Vulliez) ; Nicolaus de Dybin (by Hans Szklenar)[92] ; Thomas Sampson's works in French (by James Hassell) ; Transmundus, *Introductiones dictandi* (by Ann Dalzell) ; and a group of French and English *artes* : Peter of Blois (?), *Libellus de arte dictandi rhetorice* ; anonymous, *Flores rhetorici* ; John of Briggis, *Compilatio de arte dictandi* ; Thomas Sampson, *Modus dictandi* ; Thomas Merke, *Formula moderni et usitati dictaminis* ; Simon of Oxford (?), *Regina Rhetorica* (by Martin Camargo). As the manuscript materials become better catalogued, other editions will be undertaken.

For the reasons given in the previous chapter, the editing of dictaminal texts can be extremely difficult. In the case of a popular text, the editor is nearly always compelled to adopt a "best-text" approach, since the manuscript tradition is generally too complex to permit an accurate recension. For the same reason, a critical edition that recorded all variant readings would inevitably require an apparatus much larger than the text

[91] A late redaction of Bernard's *summa* has been edited by SAVORELLI, *Il "dictamen" di Bernardo Silvestre*, p. 182-230. Also see the small collection of letters, possibly by Bernard, edited by Virgilio PINI, *Multiplices epistole que diversis et variis negotiis utiliter possunt accomodari* (Biblioteca di "Quadrivium"), Bologna, 1969.

[92] See Hans SZKLENAR, *Magister Nicolaus de Dybin : Vorstudien zu einer Edition seiner Schriften. Ein Beitrag zur Geschichte der literarischen Rhetorik im späteren Mittelalter* (Münchener Texte und Untersuchungen zur deutschen Literatur des Mittelalters, 65), Munich, 1981, especially p. 126-180. On Nicolaus, also see Samuel P. JAFFE, *Nicolaus Dybinus' Declaracio Oracionis de Beata Dorothea : Studies and Documents in the History of Late Medieval Rhetoric*, Wiesbaden, 1974.

itself. Clearly a certain amount of selectivity is required in deciding which variants to record, particularly in texts where rapid dissemination and/or authorial revision have produced a large number of nearly contemporary but widely divergent copies. Should long extracts from a different treatise be regarded as quotation or as interpolation ? And if the contents of a later work derive from a single source, should the work be considered an abridgement of that source, no matter how thorough the revisions ? How does one decide which letters belong in a given *dictator*'s collection of models and which have been added by later copyists ? These and other questions must be answered by the prospective editor, and the answers will vary according to the specific treatise in question.

CHAPTER VI

HISTORICAL VALUE

The relevance of the *ars dictaminis* to many areas of medieval history has not escaped earlier scholars [93]. Because so much material remains in manuscript, however, the source value of the *artes dictandi* and the collections of model *dictamina* is far from exhausted.

Since all of the treatises here discussed were in some sense school texts, the most obvious value of dictaminal writings is to the historiographer of medieval education. The *ars dictaminis* evolved during the period when the first medieval universities developed from the cathedral schools, and many elements of the early history of the universities are vividly illuminated by the *artes dictandi*. The dominance of theology at Paris, for example, is consistent with the French *dictatores*' emphasis on authority (in the form of proverbs, citations from the Bible or ancient authorities) and with the status of *dictamen* as an adjunct to grammar, the most elementary discipline in the curriculum. In northern Europe, most students seem to have received their instruction in *dictamen* in the grammar schools, before they entered the university. At Bologna, by contrast, where the study of law reigned supreme, *dictamen* was studied in a more secular, practical context that promoted a more authentically rhetorical emphasis on argumentation. The Italian *dictatores* played a more prominent role in the life of their university than did their French counterparts – there were more of them, their names appear more frequently in the records, they wrote more treatises dealing with a wider variety of topics – and their status and activities say much about the organization of the university and its function within the society that created and fostered it. Because so many of the "protohumanists" were lawyers or notaries trained at Bologna or the other Italian universities that developed later, the works of the *dictatores* who trained them and who often were themselves practising notaries provide important clues to the origins of humanism.

The model letters that the *dictatores* produced in such great numbers

[93] See especially FAULHABER, *"Summa" of Guido Faba*, p. 109-111 ; SCHALLER, *"Ars dictaminis"*, col. 1038 ; and SZKLENAR, *Nicolaus de Dybin*, p. 19-28.

are also rich witnesses to the daily experience of medieval students and teachers. In them one reads about the latest academic fads and debates ; the details of university administration ; the rivalries among teachers, among different groups of students, and among factions inside and outside the academy ; the motives that drew students to the schools ; the hardships and the pleasures of student life ; and of course the constant struggle to maintain the flow of cash from relatives and patrons at home. Despite the irony, hyperbole, and exoticism that sometimes characterize the model letters, they provide a vivid and varied impression of student life [94].

Close study of the *artes* and the manuscripts that contain them also has much to reveal about the organization of curricula and the methods of teaching employed by medieval masters of arts. In both France and Italy (at least until the late thirteenth century) the *artes dictandi* point to a blurred distinction, for pedagogical purposes, between grammar and rhetoric. There is also a wide variation, often in the same school or even in the several works of a single author, in the emphasis on teaching by precept or by imitation of models. Much work remains to be done by way of clarifying the circumstances, methods, and aims of instruction in the *ars dictaminis*.

Historians of law were among the first to study the *ars dictaminis*, and for good reason. Law as an academic discipline grew up in Bologna, in close association with the *ars dictaminis* and the *ars notariae*. Many *summae dictandi* contain collections of legal documents, whether genuine or invented, often accompanied by theoretical analysis and classification of such documents and more or less detailed instructions for their preparation. Such materials reveal that the link between *dictamen* and legal studies was important in France, Germany, and England, as well as in Italy, despite the curricular differences already noted.

Because so many *dictatores* served as secretaries, notaries, or scribes in lay or ecclesiastical chanceries, and because virtually anyone charged with the preparation of official records and communications may be presumed to have had some training in the *ars dictaminis*, the *artes dictandi* are rich sources of information about administration, diplomacy, and other aspects of medieval bureaucracy. The collections of models, especially those written by prominent administrators such as Pier della

[94] See Charles H. HASKINS, *The Life of Medieval Students as Illustrated by Their Letters*, in *The American Historical Review*, 3 (1897-98), 203-229 ; revised and expanded in *Studies in Mediaeval Culture*, New York, 1929 ; reprinted New York, 1965, p. 1-35.

Vigna and Thomas of Capua, often include genuine documents of considerable historical importance. In addition to the authentic documents, many of which have already been printed, the fictional *dictamina* can also provide important information to the political historian, by recording popular reactions to contemporary events, for example.

A very promising, still largely unexplored body of information invites the social historian. The copious materials composed by the *dictatores* have much to tell us about the concerns of various social classes besides the students. Popular customs and beliefs are frequently described or invoked in the model letters and are occasionally recounted in detail, as in Boncompagno's discussion of the manner in which the various peoples of Europe mourn their dead (ed. ROCKINGER, *Briefsteller*, I : 141-143). The letter collections are rich sources of information about love and marriage ; friendship [95] ; parent-child, sibling, and other familial relationships ; death ; the religious and intellectual life ; crime and punishment ; urban and rural economies ; travel ; social hierarchies [96] ; and many other facets of medieval life. The large collections of proverbs and model *exordia* provide a primer in popular ethics, and the paired model letters, the first posing a problem for which the response offers a possible solution, mix practical advice with correct epistolary form.

Finally, the *ars dictaminis* can be a profitable area of study for historians of language and literature, both Latin and vernacular. By the late twelfth century the French *dictatores* had begun to compose fanciful exchanges modeled after the popular debate literature, and by the next generation the invented letter had become for some authors primarily a means of displaying their literary virtuosity [97]. Works such as Matthew of Vendôme's verse *Epistule*, Jean de Limoges' *Morale somnium Pharaonis*, and Boncompagno's *Rota Veneris* are atypical in being almost entirely "literary", but most *artes* contain some material of interest to the literary historian. The epistle was a favorite vehicle for imaginative literature during the Middle Ages, and both the precepts and the models in the *artes dictandi* can help illuminate its use [98].

[95] See Jean LECLERCQ, *L'Amitié dans les lettres au moyen âge*, in *Revue du moyen âge latin*, 1 (1945), 391-410.

[96] See Giles CONSTABLE, *The Structure of Medieval Society According to the 'Dictatores' of the Twelfth Century*, in *Law, Church, and Society : Essays in Honor of Stephan KUTTNER*, ed. Kenneth PENNINGTON and Robert SOMERVILLE, Philadelphia, 1977, p. 253-267.

[97] BENSON, *Protohumanism and Narrative Technique*, p. 35-36.

[98] On the love letter, for example, see Dieter SCHALLER, *Probleme der Überlieferung und*

The Italian *dictatores* had already begun to compose model letters and speeches in the vernacular a century before Dante, and the influence of this early "art prose" on the formation of literary Italian has long been recognized. Though less advanced, the study of dictaminal influence on the formation of other written vernaculars has also proved rewarding [99]. Besides discussing questions of grammatical correctness, punctuation, composition, and synonymy (for the sake of variety), the *artes dictandi* cover a wide range of stylistic concerns, including rhythm, figural language, and vices to be avoided. Much of this material is admittedly taken directly from well-known grammatical sources, but it is often applied in novel and interesting ways [100].

Verfasserschaft lateinischer Liebesbriefe des hohen Mittelalters, in *Mittellateinisches Jahrbuch*, 3 (1966), 25-36 ; Ernstpeter RUHE, *De Amasio ad Amasiam : Zur Gattungsgeschichte des mittelalterlichen Liebesbriefes* (Beiträge zur romanischen Philologie des Mittelalters, 10), Munich, 1975 ; and Martin CAMARGO, *The Verse Love Epistle : An Unrecognized Genre*, in *Genre*, 13 (1980), 397-405.

[99] See especially FAULHABER, *"Summa" of Guido Faba*, p. 110-111 (with extensive bibliography).

[100] Charles THUROT excerpts a number of *artes dictandi* in his *Notices et extraits de divers manuscrits latins pour servir à l'histoire des doctrines grammaticales au moyen âge*, in *Notices et extraits*, 22 (1868), 1-592 ; reprinted Frankfurt-am-Main, 1964.

Déjà paru :

1 : L. Genicot, *Introduction* / 1972 / 36 p. 2-503-36001-7
2 : G. Fransen, *Les décrétales et les collections de décrétales* / 1972 / 48 p. + 7 p. mise à jour 2-503-36002-5
3 : L. Genicot, *Les actes publics* / 1972 / 52 p. + 13 p. mise à jour 2-503-36003-3
4 : † N. Huygebaert, *Les documents nécrologiques* / 1972 / 76 p. + 15 p. mise à jour par J.L. Lemaitre 2-503-36004-1
5 : R. Noël, *Les dépôts de pollens fossiles* / 1972 / 96 p. + diagr. H.T. + 18 p. mise à jour 2-503-36005-x
6 : Ph. Godding, *La jurisprudence* / 1973 / 44 p. 2-503-36006-8
7 : A. Matthys, *La céramique* / 1973 / 72 p. 2-503-36007-6
8 : M. Smeyers, *La miniature* / 1974 / 124 p. + 32 p. mise à jour 2-503-36008-4
9 : A. Sempoux, *La nouvelle* / 1973 / 36 p. + 8 p. mise à jour 2-503-36009-2
10 : G. Fransen, *Les collections canoniques* / 1973 / 56 p. + 10 p. mise à jour 2-503-36010-6
11 : O. Pontal, *Les statuts synodaux* / 1975 / 100 p. 2-503-36011-4
12 : † J.-Ch. Payen & F. Dieckstra, *Le roman* / 1975 / 160 p. + 8 p. mise à jour 2-503-36012-2
13 : O. Jodogne & † J.-Ch. Payen, *Le fabliau et le lai narratif* / 1975 / 64 p. + 11 p. mise à jour 2-503-36013-0
14 : M. McCormick, *Les annales du haut moyen âge* / 1975 / 56 p. 2-503-36014-9
15 : L. Genicot, *Les généalogies* / 1975 / 44 p. + 12 p. mise à jour 2-503-36015-7
16 : K.H. Krüger, *Die Universalchroniken* / 1976 / 64 p. + 16 p. mise à jour 2-503-36016-5
17 : G. Constable, *Letters and Letter-Collections* / 1976 / 68 p. 2-503-36017-3
18 : M.-A. Arnould, *Les relevés de feux* / 1976 / 98 p. + 13 p. mise à jour 2-503-36018-1
19 : G. Despy, *Les tarifs de tonlieux* / 1976 / 48 p. 2-503-36019-X
20 : M. Pastoureau, *Les armoiries* / 1976 / 84 p. + 14 p. mise à jour 2-503-36020-3
21 : Ph. Grierson, *Les monnaies* / 1977 / 52 p. 2-503-36021-1
22 : L. Genicot, *La loi* / 1977 / 56 p. + 10 p. mise à jour 2-503-36022-X
23 : N. Coulet, *Les visites pastorales* / 1977 / 88 p. + 25 p. mise à jour 2-503-36023-8
24-25 : G. Philippart, *Les légendiers et autres manuscrits hagiographiques* / 1977 / 140 p. + 42 p. mise à jour 2-503-36024-6
26 : J. Dubois, *Les martyrologes du moyen âge latin* / 1978 / 90 p. + 9 p. mise à jour 2-503-36026-2
27 : † C. Vogel, *Les "libri paenitentiales"* / 1978 / 116 p. + 49 p. mise à jour par A.J. Frantzen 2-503-36027-0
28 : R. Fossier, *Les polyptiques et censiers* / 1978 / 72 p. 2-503-36028-9
29 : L.F. Genicot, *L'architecture. Considérations générales* / 1978 / 88 p. 2-503-36029-7
30 : C. Thiry, *La plainte funèbre* / 1978 / 92 p. + 3 p. mise à jour 2-503-36030-0
31 : A. Derolez, *Les catalogues de bibliothèques* / 1979 / 72 p. 2-503-36031-9
32 : R. Halleux, *Les textes alchimiques* / 1979 / 156 p. 2-503-36032-7
33 : M. Heinzelmann, *Translationsberichte und andere Quellen des Reliquienkultes* / 1979 /128 p. 2-503-36033-5
34 : C. Gaier, *Les armes* / 1979 / 96 p. + 10 p. mise à jour 2-503-36034-3
35 : R. Favreau, *Les inscriptions médiévales* / 1979 / 128 p. + 7 p. mise à jour 2-503-36035-1
36 : M. Pastoureau, *Les sceaux* / 1981 / 80 p. 2-503-36036-X
37 : M. Sot, *"Gesta episcoporum, gesta abbatum"* / 1981 / 60 p. + 3 p. mise à jour 2-503-36037-8
38 : J. Richard, *Les récits de voyages et de pèlerinages* / 1981 / 88 p. + 6 p. mise à jour 2-503-36038-6

39 : E. Poulle, *Les sources astronomiques : textes, tables, instruments* / 1981 / 88 p. 2-503-36039-4

40 : C. Bremond, J. Le Goff, J.-C. Schmitt, *L'"exemplum"* / 1982 / 168 p. 2-503-36040-8

41 : J. Gilissen, *La coutume* / 1982 / 122 p. 2-503-36041-6

42 : M. Pastoureau, *Jetons, méreaux et médailles* / 1985 / 48 p. 2-503-36042-4

43 : P. Brommer, *"Capitula episcoporum". Die bischöflichen Kapitularien des 9. und 10. Jahrhunderts* / 1985 / 71 p. 2-503-36044-0

44-45 : B.C. Bazàn, J.F. Wippel, G. Fransen & D. Jacquart, *Les questions disputées et les questions quodlibétiques dans les Facultés de Théologie, de Droit et de Médecine* / 1985 / 317 p. 2-503-36045-9

46 : A. de Vogüé, *Les Règles monastiques anciennes* (400-700) / 1985 / 62 p. 2-503-36046-7

47 : M. Madou, *Le costume civil* / 1986 / 67 p. 2-503-36047-5

48 : G. van Dievoet, *Les coutumiers, les styles, les formulaires et les "artes notariae"* / 1986 / 86 p. 2-503-36048-3

49 : R. Boyer, D. Bushinger, A. Crepin, J. Flori, J.-M. Paquette, F. Suard, M. Tyssens, J. Victorio, sous la direction de J. Victorio avec la collaboration de J.-C. Payen (†), *L'épopée* / 1987 / 252 p. 2-503-36049-1

50 : A. Graboïs, *Les sources hébraïques médiévales. Volume I : Chroniques, Lettres et "Responsa"* / 1987 / 96 p. 2-503-36050-5

51 : A.-D. von den Brincken, *Kartographische Quellen. Welt-, See- und Regionalkarten* / 1988 / 117 p. 2-503-36051-3

52 : M. Huglo, *Les livres de chant liturgique* / 1988 / 141 p. 2-503-36052-1

53 : A.-V. Munaut, *Les cernes de croissance des arbres (La dendrochronologie)* / 1988 / 53 p. 2-503-36053-x

54 : D.P. Blok, *Ortsnamen* / 1988 / 51 p. 2-503-36054-8

55 : J. Szövérffy, *Latin Hymns* /1989 / 141 p. 2-503-36055-6

56 : A.G. Martimort, *"Ordines", Ordinaires et cérémoniaux* / 1991 / 121 p. 2-503-36056-4

57 : P. Dinzelbacher, *Revelationes* / 1991 / 108 p. 2-503-36057-2

58 : J.O. Ward, *Ciceronian Rhetoric, Scholion and Commentary* / sous presse

59 : D. Kelly, *The Arts of Poetry and Prose* / 1991 / 180 p. 2-503-36059-9

60 : M. Camargo, *"Ars dictaminis", "Ars dictandi"* / 1991 / 59 p. 2-503-36060-2

Imprimé par les Usines Brepols S.A. - Turnhout (Belgique)
Printed in Belgium
D/1991/0095/22
ISBN 2-503-36000-9
ISBN 2-503-36060-2